CROSSROADS

THE TEENAGE GIRL'S GUIDE TO EMOTIONAL WOUNDS

GOTEE RECORDING ARTIST
Stephanie Smith
& Suzy Weibel

 ZONDERVAN®

ZONDERVAN.com/
AUTHORTRACKER
follow your favorite authors

 invert

 youth specialties

youth
specialties

Crossroads: The Teenage Girl's Guide to Emotional Wounds
Copyright 2008 by Stephanie Smith and Suzy Weibel

Youth Specialties products, 300 S. Pierce St., El Cajon, CA 92020 are published by Zondervan, 5300 Patterson Ave. SE, Grand Rapids, MI 49530.

ISBN 978-0-310-28550-2

Cover design by David Conn
Interior design by Mark Novelli, IMAGO MEDIA

Printed in the United States of America

08 09 10 11 12 13 • 20 19 18 17 16 15 14 13 12 11 10 9 8 7 6 5 4 3 2

Acknowledgments

To our families: Karen and Matt; Jonathan, Rachael, and Marie—
Thank you for walking together with us through
our collective dysfunction. Once again God showed us
the perfection of his intentional design when he chose us
one for another.

To my father—I love you. Stephanie

Contents

▶ INTRODUCTION

First we want to say thank you for picking up our book. Both of us have had "write a book" on our to-do lists for years, so we're happy to know that "read a book" was on your to-do list today.

There is, of course, a story behind this book and a reason these thoughts were put to paper. For a long time, we have both been involved with a national ministry to teens called Pure Freedom. In fact Stephanie began her affiliation with Pure Freedom as a 13-year-old retreat attendee, but her first Pure Freedom event as a featured artist took place seven years later. That's when this book really began.

During lunch with ministry founder and author Dannah Gresh, Stephanie shared the story of how she had met her father only twice and had recently penned a song about her journey toward loving and forgiving him. Dannah was moved by Stephanie's story and asked, "Do you think you could share that story and song after lunch?"

Four hundred girls got a close-up view of Stephanie's deepest pain as she performed the song "First Words" for them. Nearly one quarter of the audience—almost 100 girls—admitted that day that they had similar wounds from their fathers. As Steph came down from the stage, she saw her former youth pastor standing there. "Welcome to your ministry, Stephanie Smith," he whispered.

In the following two years, hundreds of other girls have had the opportunity to let the message of "First Words" pour hope into their hurting hearts. Two responses have been consistent: The stage fills with young women desperately seeking a way to rise above the pain "First Words" describes so poignantly. Or girls ask, "Where can I get a copy of that song?" That's where this book comes in.

Here's how the book works. While putting together Stephanie's story, we realized her debut album more or less lyrically follows the course of the very story we wanted to tell. Each chapter is therefore titled after a track on the record and begins with a sample of Stephanie's lyrics. From there each chapter delves into a bit of Stephanie's story. In the process of writing about Stephanie's life, we stumbled upon the truth that forgiveness is not the only choice we have to make in the course of our lives. We make incredibly difficult decisions every day about who we want to be and how we want to live.

Following our album theme, each chapter has

a section called "Choose Your Playlist." In this section we ask a question of you. The questions are all different, but behind each is the same decision: Are you willing to believe that God is who he says he is and that his promises of care and love and presence are true? Or are you going to believe you're stuck in a life that will never work out and that you have no choice but to be unhappy, bitter, and disconnected? That might sound a little harsh, but those really are the choices many of us have to make. Life is hard. So what are you going to do about that?

"Your Song" is a section in each chapter that asks you to take an action step. Some of these are simple and quick; some will need to be completed over time. Some are for the individual; others invite people close to you to walk alongside you. Some are fun; some may be painful. In each case we have prayerfully chosen steps we think will bring you closer to living the life God desires for you.

Finally, in "So You Want to Be a Rock Star?" we visit the stories of ordinary people who have found themselves at all kinds of crossroads. Something in their lives forced them to look long and hard into the grace of God and decide if they believed in it. We don't think we're giving away too much of the plot to tell you this: Each storyteller will offer the same truths—God is who he says he is. He is faithful. He can be trusted.

So are you ready for a hard, honest, healing journey? If so, you aren't alone. Though the pieces of this story unfold through the life of one person, it is not the Stephanie Smith extravaganza. This is your story; it's our story; it's the story of life.

▶ LAST WORDS

> Then Jesus came to them and said, "All authority in heaven and on earth has been given to me. Therefore go and make disciples of all nations, baptizing them in the name of the Father and of the Son and of the Holy Spirit, and teaching them to obey everything I have commanded you. **And surely I am with you always, to the very end of the age."**
>
> (Matthew 28:18-20, emphasis added)

Life is hard. This book could end right now because, frankly, that's one of life's great secrets, and now that you know it, there might not be a whole lot left to say. It is seriously tough out there in the world. I don't want to depress anybody right off the bat, but if you pay any attention at all, you know what I'm talking about. I guess we have to consider the very real possibility that these are simply the last days referred to by the apostle Paul in one of his letters to his friend Timothy—you can read his words for yourself in 2 Timothy 3:1-5. But I have to warn you, it's not encouraging news.

I don't know what your hardship is, but I'm willing to go out on a limb and say you have known trouble in your life. If not, I probably need to take your pulse. Here are some statistics to consider: Nearly 20 percent of Americans report having experienced some form of sexual abuse in their childhood years (Advocates for Youth). 60 percent of Americans are overweight, and 34 percent are considered obese (ANRED). Studies reveal that almost 40 percent of marriages end in divorce (Americans for Divorce Reform). With numbers like these, chances are very good that, like me, you grew up as a statistic of some sort.

My statistic is one of fatherlessness. Did you know that nearly one-third of young Americans have moved into adulthood without a father present (fathersforlife.org)? If you are fatherless too, the statistics say something about your "likelihoods." They say you are 6.6 times more likely than other kids to become a teenage parent. They say you are also 6.6 times more likely to drop out of school, and 15 times more likely to end up in prison while still a teenager. They say you are five times more likely to take your own life (fathersforlife.org). There are other statistics about rape, running away, and behavioral disorders, but none of them are happy.

This is not a book intended to depress anyone. No, this is a book about hope. So let's begin with a big statistic rejection party. Now, I'm not stupid enough to think that statistics have no validity. I understand that most of them have been gathered and weighed in some scientific manner that I don't totally understand. I do understand statistics represent a version of reality. But I believe the reality they represent is one-sided. They show us a reality without hope, without possibility, without Christ.

The statistics are one voice. But God's voice is something else entirely. And the kind of life you have depends on which of those two voices you listen to. From the beginning God has been about beating the odds. Are you ready for my awesome literary device? The first words in this chapter are from Matthew 28:20, "And surely I am with you always, to the very end of the age." These are the last words spoken by Jesus before he ascended into heaven to begin his reign at the right hand of God. See? The first words are the last words. Clever, right? This actually has a greater significance than my own literary cleverness, though.

Before Jesus' death on the cross and resurrection from the dead, people believed God's presence dwelled in a part of the tabernacle called the Holy of Holies. They believed only the holiest of people—a High Priest—could come into the presence of God. And even the High Priest was terrified at the prospect. It was believed that no one could look upon God and live. This belief created some strange problems. For instance, if for any reason the priest were struck dead while in the Holy of Holies, no one else could come in to retrieve his body. So he would enter the room with a rope tied about his ankle. Then if he committed a deadly faux pas, his buddies could simply pull his body out of there.

As Jesus was completing his years of ministry on earth, he was clear that he was God made flesh. People went to ridiculous extremes to be near him—cutting holes in the roofs of homes, climbing trees, diving for the hem of his robe. He was the original rock star.

Scene change. It's late afternoon, and the sun beats down upon three men cruelly hung on Roman crosses. Blood and sweat mingle on the bodies of the crucified men as their strength wanes with each passing second. Suddenly the man in the middle, who moments ago seemed lifeless, cries out in a loud voice, *"Eloi, Eloi, lama sabachthani?* (My God, my God, why have you forsaken me?)"* A sudden darkness blankets the land as if the sun has been snuffed out by the very hand of God. A quake shakes the foundations of the earth. And then in the Holy of Holies, the curtain that, for hundreds of years, was a sign of the separation between humans and God is cleanly ripped in two. It falls heavily to the floor and—no one dies. The separation is no more. "It is finished," Jesus cried. Humanity is reconciled to its Creator.

This book tells the story of my relationship with my dad, whom I didn't even meet until I was 14 years old. Go figure that one out. I know firsthand how important a dad is to a girl because I grew up with a huge, gaping hole in my world, and our relationship needed some serious reconciliation.

I sometimes joke around with my friends that I'm the little bird from P.D. Eastman's *Are You My Mother?* (I actually just like to make the face of that confused little birdie.) But growing up without a dad, I often felt just as discombobulated as that little guy. In the story the bird has no idea what a mother is—he was separated from her before he could grow any mom associations. He ends up asking random things—a cow, an airplane, and a steam shovel—if they are his mother.

In the same way I really didn't know what a dad was. I had invented a fairy-tale guy in my head, but beyond the basics that I wanted to know—did I look like him? laugh like him?—I had never grown any dad associations. I had watched my friends with their dads, but none of them could adequately answer the question of what my dad would have meant to me. Could he have convinced me I was beautiful? Would I have been more involved in school if he were around? Would he have made me feel protected? Would I trust men more if he had been there to show me how an honorable man acts? Like that little bird, I had no idea what to look for.

I was on my way to fulfilling a number of those other "fatherless" statistics several times. I'll tell those stories in this book. But I want these first words to reveal who I am today. I don't want to make you wait, and I don't want to leave you guessing.

My hope is that people know that what they see is what they get with me. I value realness as much as anybody else in my generation. I am sometimes needy, sometimes profound, sometimes silly, sometimes deep and sensitive, and sometimes in need of a stern reality check from people who love me. I don't want you to think I've arrived yet. In the big picture it all comes back to those last words. While the world often seems to have little room for anything other than bitterness and division, I see God leading me—and you—in another direction.

To stay bitter is too easy, and there's a part of me that resents "too easy." How about you? I'm not one of those people who want a head start in a race. I don't want my opponent to let me win. And I'm in if God says, "I'm going to do this great thing for you, but it's not going to be easy. It might take a while."

In all of our trials, in all of our tribulations, in our heartaches and our brokenness, God is there. We have a choice: We can walk with God, or we can walk away from him. We have been given authority. We have been assigned purpose. We were slaves, but now we are free.

Too often we bow to statistics, standards, and norms as if they are the only way the pendulum of our lives can swing. I want you to know the truth. Jesus said it: "I have told you these things, so that in me you may have peace. In this world you will have trouble. But take heart! I have overcome the world" (John 16:33). At every crossroads you have a choice. Some people choose to take heart and believe the promise that Jesus has won. Others choose a life of futility, always trying to script the end of a story that has already been written.

Which way will you go at that crossroads? This book is rich with stories—some are mine; some belong to other people. All of them point the way to the promises of God. They are sometimes raw stories, written by broken and vulnerable people just like you and me. These are the stories of my rock star friends. Most play no instruments. Most have no national stage. They are simply people who have decided to let love be loud and to rock whatever circumstances God has given them. I hope that in these stories you, too, will find the courage to win.

should have killed him. It didn't. Instead, it caused a stroke that led to severe physical damage. After months in the hospital, Jeff was able to come home where he began slowly—very, very slowly—to recover.

My reaction to whammy number two was different. I believed God could bring good out of this difficult situation and I needed to look for that good. That was easy to do in my head, but I didn't realize how much work the Lord had yet to do in my heart.

On many days I questioned why Jeff had to struggle so much. But other times—and it's hard to admit this—much of my frustration and anger and prayer that Jeff would be healed had nothing to do with him. I wanted him to get better because I wanted things to be easier for me.

One day I was running late for an appointment, as usual. Jeff sat on the steps waiting patiently for me to tie his shoes and move him to his wheelchair. As I knelt to tie his shoes, resentment and anger welled up in me. Inwardly I yelled at God, *I shouldn't have to be doing this. He's 10 years old. I shouldn't have to tie his shoes anymore.* I screamed inside my head as I roughly pulled the laces, *I hate this.*

Unexpectedly I heard the Lord's voice quietly reply, *I didn't enjoy going to the cross either, Leah. But I did it gladly for you.* I suddenly saw my anger for what it was: selfishness and pride. Weeping, I confessed, "Lord Jesus, if I have to tie Jeff's shoes for the rest of his life and mine, let me do it gladly for you."

That was 12 years ago. Today Jeff uses a power wheelchair. He has no use of his left hand, but God gave him the strength and patience to work hard on his recovery. He now attends a Christian college and is preparing for full-time ministry. Most of the time he's able to wear shoes with a nifty Velcro strap, but there are still days when I have the privilege of tying his shoes.

SO YOU WANT TO BE A ROCK STAR?

Putting Life's Plans on Hold
by Kari Lucas

On June 4, 2004, my life and what I thought it was going to be completely changed. At age 19, I was diagnosed with leukemia. I had completed my freshman year of college, and everything seemed perfect. I had a great summer job and spent time with my friends every evening. My family was healthy—and apart from having a few weird bruises, I felt healthy, too. A Division I softball player at Penn State, I was working out hard five to six days a week even though it was the off-season. My life was good. Until the evening I was diagnosed with cancer.

Never did I believe this would happen to me. I ate healthy food, worked out daily, and took care of my body. But there it was—cancer. I spent the whole next day refusing to believe I was sick. Within 12 hours of my diagnosis, however, I started my first chemotherapy treatment.

There was no turning back. I had to fight this in order to live. I was given a five-month calendar of how my life would be. It was planned out day-by-day, treatment-by-treatment. People would tell me they didn't think they'd be able to go through something like this. I'd smile and say, "Yes, you would, because you would have no other choice."

I was in the Hershey Medical Center for 87 days, going through four rounds of chemotherapy to kill the cancer. It was one of the toughest experiences I have endured thus far. It was also one of the best. I lost my hair, but I never lost my faith in God.

I am lucky to have grown up in a Christian family. We attended church regularly, but I never knew how much I needed God until I was fighting for my life. Many Christians told me it was okay to be angry and upset with God, but I never was. God instilled a peace within me, and somehow I knew everything was going to be all right.

When you gets sick it's tempting to ask, "Why me?" But I found myself asking, "Why not me?" I'm no more special than anyone else. I considered myself lucky to be able to battle something and come out of it stronger and healthier than ever. I feel so blessed to have grown closer to God during my experience.

I also grew close to many other cancer patients, who ranged in age from two to 24. Age doesn't matter much when you're fighting for your life. We were like crutches for each other, fighting our battles together. My doctors and nurses were also my heroes and guardian angels. My family was my rock. I was truly blessed throughout this entire process.

This experience was extremely difficult for my parents. They wanted to protect me, but they couldn't do a thing about my cancer. I tried to show them I believed I was going to be okay and God had a plan for me. I just knew I had too much left to do, too much life left to live. I also knew this experience would help me with my true passion: working with people.

I was declared in remission on October 14, 2004, and I began to get my life back together. During my treatment, I'd tried to keep in shape as much as I could, but the chemo really took a toll on my body, muscles, and my ability to work out. I could only walk a few steps a day. So I knew it would take a lot of work to get back into shape for softball.

When I went back to school, I wanted to prove to myself and to others that I could return to my old athletic self in three months. I have never worked as hard for something in my life. The first time I stepped onto the track after cancer was one to remember. I stood there with my bald head, my running shoes laced up, and a dream filling my heart. I wanted to run a lap without stopping. I did it, but it was so much harder than I expected. I crossed the line, put my hands on my knees and cried. This was going to be even harder than I imagined. Each day I added a lap, and each day I pushed myself harder. Finally I was ready to go, just in time for softball season.

Now I smile remembering what a challenge it

was—a challenge I am grateful I had to face. When your life is put on hold, a lot of things are put into perspective. When I was in the hospital I made lists upon lists of things I would be doing if I weren't confined to my hospital bed. Now I never sit still. I probably drive people crazy with all the energy I have, but I wouldn't want it any other way. I love to stay up late and wake up extra early. I try not to worry about little things, and I never want to take a day for granted. My life is a gift from God, but it took almost losing it to know just how precious it is. Having cancer was one of the best things that could have happened to me.

TRACK ONE: "Not Afraid"

TRACK ONE: "Not Afraid"

> So I'm not afraid to walk away
>
> Let me go for the last time
>
> Finally got it straight for the first time
>
> Not afraid cause I know he's there to meet me
>
> So I'll be gone, I'll be gone,
>
> But not alone, alone, alone

My mom never intended to leave my dad.

In her mind his abuse was somehow a small piece of a bigger picture. Sure Dad would get mad and hit her or yell at her now and then. But she'd think about all those days he would disappear for hours at a time to seek God in prayer, about those Bible verses that said she should submit to him and that he was the head of the household. It was all pretty confusing to her. When you're in the middle of being hurt, sometimes you're the last one to see it.

Mom had sought help three times before she made her final decision. The first time she went to a pastor who told her she must be doing something wrong—otherwise her husband wouldn't be so angry with her all the time. He counseled her to go home, ask forgiveness, and make a list of the things she could change so my dad wouldn't want to hit her anymore. It didn't work.

The second pastor said all that my mom needed to do was speak positive words about her marriage and God would heal it. It didn't work.

Not long after that my parents got into yet another argument over something insignificant—but loud enough to make my older brother, Matt, squirm right out of his high chair. When Mom went to grab Matt, my dad grabbed her. In his rage his hands went around her throat. My mom ended up on the floor with bad rug burns on her elbows and bruises on her neck. And Matt learned one of his first full sentences: "Mommy kick Daddy."

The next day my mom went to see a third pastor for help.

"I'm not sure I can help you," he said matter-of-factly. "I mean, I can help you, but I don't think I can help your situation."

Wow. For the first time my mom got a different glimpse of her marriage. For the first time she began to realize that some problems can't be fixed with words or by some kind of behavioral assignment from a kind counselor.

"I think a little time of separation would be wise," the pastor said. "You're a nutritionist, right?"

My mother nodded.

"You need some spiritual and emotional nutrition right now. Where can you get that?"

My grandparents bought my mom plane tickets right away. At first my dad supported the idea too, but as the time for Mom to go grew closer, he became afraid. It seemed to him they should be able to work things out at home. On the morning of her flight, he grudgingly helped Mom lift one suitcase from under the bed.

One suitcase.

Fifty dollars.

Two kids under age two.

That's all my mom had when she left town.

I spent the rest of my life growing up in Pennsylvania without my dad. Ultimately Mom made the choice to save three lives rather than ruin four.

CHOOSE YOUR PLAYLIST:
BLESSINGS OR CURSES?

In all the years I spent watching my mom sacrifice for Matt and me, there was one thing noticeably missing: I never heard my mom say anything negative about my dad. She made a choice right away that she would say nice things or say nothing at all.

I was a baby when we left. I didn't remember anything about my dad, but I had an intense loyalty to him. Because Mom never said bad things—in fact, she'd often tell me what a great golfer he was or how he held the record at the country club for holding his breath under water the longest—I had an image of a prince in my head. My dad suffered from schizophrenia—something I didn't learn until I was much older—and my mom never used his illness against him. It might sound strange, but this was a gift my mom gave to me. I didn't have a dad in my house, but I had one in my heart.

Kids have little control over how one parent speaks about another. When I was young I was completely at my mom's mercy as to how I pictured my dad. She had to decide if she wanted me to hate him or not, if I would have blessings or curses flowing into my little ears. I've come to find out that it makes a big difference.

A friend of mine defines a curse as "words spoken toward an enemy, backed by some kind of power and intended to bring hardship to the receiver."

There are many examples of curses spoken in the Bible—some are spoken by people and some by God. Maybe you're familiar with the story in the Gospel of Mark about Jesus cursing a fig tree so that it would never bear fruit again. It goes like this: "The next day as they were leaving Bethany, Jesus was hungry. Seeing in the distance a fig tree in leaf, he went to find out if it had any fruit. When he reached it, he found nothing but leaves, because it was not the season for figs. Then he said to the tree, 'May no one ever eat fruit from you again.' And his disciples heard him say it" (Mark 11:12-14).

If we break down the previous definition of a curse and apply it to what Jesus did, here's how it works out:

Words spoken toward an enemy: Maybe it's hard to imagine a tree as an enemy, but Jesus was actually using this tree as a living story. On the outside it looked like it was full of fruit—a pretty deceptive temptation for a hungry man. But why say the tree was an enemy? In this case the tree represented the nation of Israel (the fig tree was often used as a metaphor for the Hebrew people). Some of these people whose ancestors had followed God for centuries rejected Jesus as the Messiah. Jesus often compared those people—and their religion that seemed righteous and proper but was really full of hypocrisy—to cups that are clean on the outside but dirty on the inside (Matthew 23:25) and tombs that look pristine, but hold decaying bodies (Matthew 23:27-28). In the same way the fig tree looked good, but it had nothing to offer.

Backed by some kind of power: Jesus cursed the fig tree as he was going to Jerusalem for his final week of ministry on earth. His disciples were about to learn what it meant to be persecuted; they needed to know their enemies were not as powerful as their Lord. Check out what happened. "In the morning, as they went along, they saw the fig tree withered from the roots. Peter remembered and said to Jesus, 'Rabbi, look! The fig tree you cursed has withered!'" (Mark 11:20-21).

Intended to bring hardship: The obvious hardship to this poor little tree was that its healthy leaves and roots withered, eventually causing the tree to die. Jesus promised his disciples at this moment that whatever they asked for in his name he would do for them.

Curses are serious business, and many of us suffer under them every day. We are subject to all kinds of statements that are said to and about us, intended to bring us some kind of harm. Think about all of the potential curses you have heard— and maybe even spoken:

"You are so stupid!"

"Why can't you do anything right?"

"You'll never amount to anything!"

"I wish you had never been born."

"I hate you!"

When curses land on us—or when we toss them out at others—there are some pretty negative results. We lose the ability to see the good in other people. We stop believing we are capable of goodness. We turn into people no one wants to be around. We become depressed, isolated, distrustful, alienated, and miserable.

I know you'd never choose any of those hurtful feelings for yourself, but what do you do when you're young and they are chosen for you? If you hear "you are so stupid" often enough, you just might become convinced. And if one parent constantly tells you what a total idiot the other parent is, you might start to believe it—that's a real tragedy. It doesn't even matter if there's a little bit of truth in the statements. Only seeing the worst in others, only hearing the worst about yourself makes for a sad, lonely life.

My mom knew that the answer to the curse is the blessing. A blessing might be described as "affirmation for the recipient through promises of hope and God's goodness."

Doesn't that sound infinitely better than a curse? In Old Testament culture, blessings—from God, from parents, from the religious community—were ferociously sought after. Joseph received blessing from his father, Jacob, and it drove his older brothers to such jealous distraction that they kidnapped him and sold him into slavery.

We don't think much about blessings these days, but I think we should. So let's break down that definition:

Protection for the recipient: I want protection in my life. That may be one of the biggest reasons I created an entire fairy tale that revolved around the dad I had never known. Little did I know that my mom was actually providing me with one of the greatest protections possible. It wasn't physical, though I think she would have tried to wipe the floor with anyone who tried to hurt me (and you should see my mom—all five feet four inches of her). No, she was teaching me the emotionally protective power of blessing.

Jesus taught his followers a twist on blessings and Old Testament law when he said to them, "But to you who are listening I say: Love your enemies, do good to those who hate you, bless those who curse you, pray for those who mistreat you" (Luke 6:27-28). Blessings cancel out curses. Author Frank Hammond says it this way: "Did it ever occur to you to bless your enemies? This is God's way of protecting yourself from curses spoken out against you. If, on the other hand, you have bitterness, unforgiveness, hatred, and anger in your heart against your antagonist, you are making a landing strip for the curse to alight" (Hammond, 2).

Promises of hope and God's goodness: A blessing carries a promise, and it always holds the same underlying promise—God is who he says he is. In the Bible blessings were spoken for health, for inheritance, and for children, and the promise was always the same—God is present, God is good, God is God. God is able to do infinitely more than we could ever imagine or ask him to do. His goodness is so great we can't even fully understand it. There is no equal.

Nothing has brought more hope into my life than this simple truth: God is and forever will be God. He does not change, and he cannot lie. So how can he be anything other than all of his amazing qualities that we constantly see at work around us—love, joy, grace, compassion? When we know for certain that this truly is the character of God and when we accept that he has loved us with an everlasting love, how can we look to our future with anything but hope?

In Deuteronomy God gives blessings and curses other names, saying through Moses: "This day I call the heavens and the earth as witnesses against you that I have set before you life and death, blessings and curses. Now choose life, so that you and your children may live and that you may love the LORD your God, listen to his voice, and hold fast to him" (Deuteronomy 30:19-20).

When I was young I didn't realize how my mom had chosen life over death for me. Yes, she physically rescued me from a life with an abusive man. Even greater than that, she taught me to choose life over death. Blessings over curses.

I'm still pretty young, but I've been around long enough to know this: Not many people practice speaking blessings. We are much more experienced with speaking curses. Maybe there are people speaking blessings over you; maybe not. Either way, it's important for you to set a new standard with your life. You need to become a speaker of blessings because when you speak them, you counteract the curses in your life and the lives of others. Your words send God's hope to hurting hearts.

 ## Your song

I want to give you an exercise I think might help you to choose blessings over curses, but it's going to take a few weeks—maybe even a few months. Are you up for it?

I read about this pastor in Kansas City, Missouri, who developed a system to stop saying negative things. He put a purple bracelet on one wrist and set a goal for himself: He was going to go 21 days without complaining. If he slipped and complained, he had to switch the bracelet to the other wrist and start counting again. He figured it would be easy, but he broke three bracelets before he made it to 21 days—it took him almost three months.

A bracelet, a ring—I don't care if you want to wear the same pink sock until you succeed, switching feet every time you need to. How about giving it a try, though? See if you can go 21 days speaking only blessings toward the person who has hurt you or abandoned you, the one who has really wreaked havoc in your life. Remember, to speak a blessing is not the same as saying the other person's behavior is right. My mom simply said good things that were true about my dad and chose not to verbalize the bad. You can do the same.

And remember, too, that a blessing is so much more than simply a nice word. Blessings reveal the attitudes of our hearts. In some cases a blessing might not include speaking at all. It might be walking away from a fight rather than engaging in one. It might mean approaching an old problem with a new question. It might mean taking time to look around and see if others are hurting. It truly is better to give than to receive; maybe you will find your pain lessened by the simple act of giving someone else comfort.

How long will it take to make blessing a habit? I don't know, but I know that if you want to choose life, it's the only way to go.

SO YOU WANT TO BE A ROCK STAR?
On Parents Splitting Up: Take 1
by Kylene Young

I had severe strep throat the week my mom told me she was leaving my dad. I remember every second of that phone call. I was outside by my car; I leaned on it and slid down to the ground, overwhelmed by sickness and despair. I remember screaming at her and calling her a nasty name in the midst of a slew of other profanities. This was not the reaction anyone would have expected from a Bible college student in her second year studying youth ministry.

I thought I had all of the tools necessary to deal with such a situation, but the shock of my mom's decision was a weight I didn't know how to bear. I didn't know how to properly deal with my anger toward my mom. I am ashamed to confess that every conversation I had with my mom during the next year was laced with hatred and a holier-than-thou attitude meant to make her feel guilty about seeking a divorce. It got to a point where our conversations were so strained that we couldn't talk about anything personal without me having another fit of anger.

My conversations with my dad were a bit kinder, but I was uncomfortable being his shoulder to cry on. As a proverbial "Daddy's girl," I didn't know how to bear my father's pleas, his flood of tears. My older brother, who lived in the same town as both of my parents, had to take on the burden of being the confidante for both Mom and Dad. I lived 600 miles away and persisted in my hatred toward my mom for almost two years.

I hated the way I felt—about my parents and about myself. It's no fun to be so filled with rage and self-pity. I was awful to be around. I was crabby, angry, and full of pride over how noble I was to call out my mother on her "sin."

Eventually I realized I had to make a choice: I could allow my anger to ruin my relationship with my mom and my witness for Christ, or I could accept God's command to honor our parents. I knew I had to forgive my mom.

It wasn't easy. I constantly prayed for God to help me forgive her. I even fasted, hoping I would get the clarity I needed to move past my anger. And I began to realize that forgiveness isn't a one-time thing. I have to choose forgiveness every day. When I do, my heart feels better.

My relationship with my mom has flourished since God so graciously opened my eyes to my sin of unforgiveness. And while I still pray every day that God will bring my parents back together, I continue to see the ways that God has brought good despite my parents' divorce. I am a more gracious person. I am closer to both of my parents than ever. And I know that God is always with me, even when I'm at my worst.

SO YOU WANT TO BE A ROCK STAR?

On Parents Splitting Up: Take 2
by Tim Shutes

Stunned. There's no better word to describe how I felt. I was fresh out of college, an idealistic, bright, young, know-it-all youth pastor only weeks into my new job when the unthinkable happened.

It was Valentine's Day, three weeks before my 24th birthday, when my mom told me she was leaving my dad. They say I'm lucky because I wasn't a kid when it happened. In many ways they're right. God spared my sister and me a lot of psychological baggage, but I can't say it was any easier because I was older. It was just—different.

Therapists say, "Don't get caught in the middle." Well, I got caught in the middle. My sister was in school in South Carolina. I was 10 minutes from home. Suddenly I was the stable one, and instead of focusing on my brand new ministry, I was pulling overtime as a marriage counselor for my parents. I found myself going back and forth between desperately sharing my father's grief and uttering cold clichés to my mother in hope that something would stick and make everything better.

I thought life was supposed to be different. People aren't supposed to get divorced after 26 years of marriage, especially not Christians, especially not my parents. My dad was an emotional wreck, and my mom seemed like a different person altogether. I pleaded with God to rescue their marriage. In my idealistic world God always brought couples back together. How could a God who hates divorce not make that happen for my parents?

The truth is that if my parents had gotten back together right away, it would have short-circuited all the ways my family—me included—grew because of this painful situation. You see, living in the daily tragedy of divorce does something to a person—it first makes them numb, and then it reveals issues and sins that have been hidden for a long time. That's where I found God working on me and the rest of my family. Even in the midst of something God hates, God was present and working to bring about something good.

God says, "My people have committed two sins: They have forsaken me, the spring of living water, and have dug their own cisterns, broken cisterns that cannot hold water" (Jeremiah 2:13). My parents' relationship was a broken cistern that I kept trying to fill and refill, only to watch it run dry. They had been my source of security, my source of stability. But they were—and are—broken people like all of us. They simply couldn't be everything I wanted them to be.

It took me a long time to realize that I can't

change my parents. I can only change myself. And because of God's goodness, I have indeed changed. God shattered my cookie-cutter faith and replaced it with a world-worn, real-life version that I would never trade. Because of this trial I am not afraid of uncertainty and change anymore. The situation forced me to confront my fears and hurts, and I am a stronger man because of it. So many people forsake God when tragedy hits. But I would have never made it without God. C.S. Lewis wrote, "God whispers to us in our pleasures, speaks to us in our conscience, but shouts in our pains" (Lewis, 93). I believe that's true. I have come to realize that as much as my heart breaks for my parents, God's heart breaks even more. God has comforted me with his tears, counseled me through his Word, and fortified me through this fiery trial.

I still have much brokenness, but I would never trade these wounds. They are reminders of how God is faithfully restoring my soul.

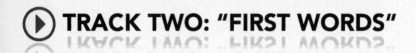

▶ TRACK TWO: "FIRST WORDS"

> But now I'm here,
> I know it's been a few years,
> I've shed a few tears, and now I have a few
> things to say
> When we met you broke my heart
> Fourteen years old and you tore me apart
> But that aside, please know I love you
> And more than that…
> I forgive you

I knew he was my dad right away. Mom said he had put on a lot of weight and she only recognized the voice, but I knew from all the way across the crowded room. The height. That dark hair slicked back. And he looked like me. Or I looked like him I guess—that's the way it genetically works.

A family funeral took us down to Louisiana, and I had wondered all the way there if I finally would meet my dad. I was 14, and my dream potentially could come true. When we arrived my mom asked the question I was afraid to put into words.

"Will Scott be coming?" she asked his brothers.

"I don't know," he said. "He didn't answer any of my phone calls. Frankly, I don't know where he is right now."

It was almost time for the funeral to begin when Mom heard his big voice booming from the front of the room and I caught my first glimpse of my dad. He eventually looked our way, and we could almost see his thoughts playing out on his face. *Well, that's Karen. Two kids. Boy and a girl. Yep. Gotta be mine.* And he made his way across the room to where we nervously waited.

He addressed my mom first. "Karen." Mom nodded back her greeting.

He then looked my brother in the eye. His handshake was firm. Masculine. "Matthew." Matt grimaced in return.

It finally was my turn. My fairy tale was about to become real. "You must be Priscilla," he said.

I went numb. This was my dad, right? The guy who helped my mom name me on the day I was born? He thinks my name is Priscilla? No offense to any Priscillas out there, but that just might have been the worst name he could have used—sorry Ms. Presley.

Without even a moment to process what had just happened, the family was called to the front for the start of the funeral. My dad actually followed us to our row and sat with us. Fortunately I was placed right next to a box of soft, inviting Kleenex, which I proceeded to empty during the next hour. I must have looked like the world's most loyal grandchild.

In truth I was the world's most heartbroken daughter. I'd been waiting my whole life to meet this man, my prince, my hero. But he didn't even know my name.

CHOOSE YOUR PLAYLIST: FIGHT OR FLIGHT?

My mom tried to comfort me after the funeral by telling me that Dad had forgotten her name, too—one week after their wedding. He had tried to introduce his new bride to someone and had just drawn a blank. I suppose that sounds awful to you. Well, it didn't help me much at the moment.

Names are supposed to be important, right? They convey a meaning. They are how we are known and how we know one another. They hold associations. Just fill in the blanks in this sentence to see what I mean:

I will never name my child _____

because of _____.

I had played out the moment I'd meet my dad so many times before. The reality was nothing like what I had imagined. I was whisked away to the front of that sanctuary as "Priscilla" before I had a chance to ask him even one question. But none of that mattered any longer, really. Not if he didn't know me. Not if he didn't know my name.

My mom says right before we began that long walk to the front of the church, she could see that I was trying to figure out what I wanted to do. I remember that moment, too. If I could have let you inside my thoughts at that exact moment, you would have heard something like this: *I have to do something. Now. I have to go somewhere. I have to move. Okay, think. I could run to the bathroom where I would be free to scream and kick at random pieces of metal, porcelain, and tile. That's what I want to do! Or, I can hold it together just long enough to get to a seat up front. I don't have to hold on to this. I don't have to be Priscilla. I am Stephanie. Mom knows I'm Stephanie. Matt knows. All of my friends back home know.*

It was an incredibly hard choice. A lot of people knew my name, but not the one I wanted to hear say Stephanie. On that day I had to choose whether I was going to hold on to this hurt that had assailed me from out of the blue or remember everything I had known just one day earlier.

Sometimes when hurt blindsides us, we react like wounded animals. Feeling cornered and taken by surprise, it is only natural to want to take out our claws and put a good scratch on our attacker. But wait a minute. That's not how animals think. That's how humans think.

When an animal is wounded, it doesn't strike out with the intent to harm. I know that sounds crazy, but animals don't possess cognitive reasoning skills. An animal strikes out to create an escape route and hopefully to save its own life—not for revenge or justice.

At that funeral I wanted an escape route. I wanted the hurt and the shame of not being known to disappear. I wanted someone to fill in this dear man on the past 14 years of my life, the time he had missed—or at least to inform him of my name. I had hoped he dreamed of meeting me, and I dreamed that when we finally did meet, he would be as well-rehearsed as I was.

Life usually doesn't work out as neatly as in our plans or dreams. Have you noticed that? It has a way of disappointing and blindsiding us. It has the ability to knock the breath out of us and steal away dreams that were lifelike only moments before.

No one knew this better than the king of recovery—a guy named Job. Imagine this poor guy. One moment he is rich beyond measure and the next his messengers bring these bits of news:

- Your oxen and donkeys have all been stolen. The servants caring for them have been slaughtered. I am the only one who survived.

- Your sheep and shepherds just got toasted by fire that fell from the sky. I'm the only one who survived.

- Your camels just got hijacked. All who tended them are dead. I'm the only one who survived.

- Your sons and daughters were all partying together when a great wind took the house down. I am the only one who survived.

That is a bad day. Oh, then Job broke out with a painful skin disease all over his body. On top of all that, Job's wife (whom God so generously left alive) told him to curse God and die.

Job had a choice to make. I guess you could argue that Job's wife offered him one valid option. Be the wounded animal. Strike out in your pain and confusion. Curse God. Go ahead, Job, play the part of the dying dog.

Personally, I'm kind of glad Job chose another option.

Job knew one cold, hard fact about God. God is good. Whatever God does is motivated by love. Since the New Testament hadn't been written when Job was alive, he didn't have this Scripture to cling to at that time, but Romans 8:28 says, "And we know that in all things God works for the good of those who love him, who have been called according to his purpose."

There is no doubt that at the moment my dad called me Priscilla, I would have struggled to tell you how God was ever going to make that work for good. (I could tell you now, but I don't want to give away the ending.) Likewise, Job stammered a bit when his friends began insisting he explain why God had done all of this to him. But from the very beginning of his trials, Job managed to say, "The LORD gave and the LORD has taken away; may the name of the LORD be praised" (Job 1:21).

I wish I could tell you that I had already figured out all of this at age 14, but that wasn't even close to being true. Maybe I chose not to run only to honor the sanctity of a funeral. It was a pretty nightmarish event all around, so maybe I was frozen and couldn't run, the way you are in bad dreams. Or maybe God was whispering to me even at that tender age, telling me that I only needed to take that first tenuous step toward goodness and he would take care of the rest.

Your song

Have you ever refused to do something because you were afraid? To the rest of the world it may have looked like you were simply being rebellious or angry. You fold your arms; your face becomes a hard, unapproachable mask. But you know the truth. You are not a rebel, an anarchist, or a snob. You are afraid.

Fear can be a paralyzing emotion. It holds us rooted where we are—even if it's a deadly place—rather than letting us move on to places where we can grow and impact the world around us. And let's face it, we all want to impact the world around us.

Is there a situation that has left you limping? Someone you need to talk to so you can straighten out a misunderstanding? Someone you need to ask for forgiveness? Facing those problems is always—let me say that again—always going to beat tucking your tail and running.

But you don't want to do this alone or unprepared. Find someone who loves you and who you know is willing to pray with you. Tell her about this bump in your relationship road and let her breathe courage into you. Next have her help you arrange a meeting with the person you need to talk to; in certain cases you might want her to go with you as a mediator. If nothing else, ask her to hold you accountable for saying and doing all that you need to say and do.

SO YOU WANT TO BE A ROCK STAR?

When Dad Never Says "I Love You"
by Andy Mylin

I had been married almost seven years the day I sat in the front seat of an old Dodge truck having one of those conversations nobody ever really wants to have. You see, God had been working on my heart for months prior to this event. He had been revealing junk that had been hiding inside me since childhood.

My mom and dad were never married to each other, but they lived together on a farm in central Pennsylvania. When I was five there was a barn fire. We didn't have insurance and lost almost everything we needed to make a living. There was no money, but Mom didn't know that. She did realize the relationship wasn't going anywhere, so she enrolled in nursing school to try to find a way to support and raise my sister, Brenda, and me. She graduated in the top two percent—not just of her class, but of the nation. Dad didn't know that. They had simply stopped communicating. Soon after her graduation mom moved out, taking Brenda and me with her.

At first I saw little of my dad who still lived in our old farmhouse—Thanksgivings and Christmases mostly. But as I got older, I became more useful around the farm and eventually spent my summer vacations there. There wasn't a better place for a young boy to grow up. I thought the world of my dad, and he taught me a great deal during that time, such as how to shoot a shotgun, how to fix things and work with my hands, how to take pride in my work and do a job right the first time.

Unfortunately there was also a negative side to our relationship. There often were long periods of time when Dad was silent. When he did speak it was condemning, derogatory. He nicknamed me "Blockhead" and used the title enough that I started to believe I couldn't do anything right. As a young man who longed for his father's approval, it was deeply hurtful to wonder if he only felt negatively about me. He never showed me much affection, and he never told me he loved me. I truly didn't know if he even liked me.

Through high school and college, I spent what time I could with Dad. But something else was happening. God consistently brought men into my life who filled the places in my heart my dad had left empty. These were godly men who challenged and encouraged me to live a life of integrity, one that reflected God's grace. They praised me and celebrated with me when I got it right and gently guided me when I got it wrong.

My story has its share of pain, but I believe it's been a story about God's blessings. God used these men to walk me through a long journey of changing how I saw myself. They trained me to see myself the way God sees me—not as a blockhead, but as his son whom he loves and is proud of.

I tell you all this to set the stage for that day sitting in the truck. It began as a miserable moment because, up to that time, there was a small part of me that still wanted Dad's approval. I wanted him to approve of my wife, the career I'd chosen—pretty much every decision I'd made. Somehow that desire had given my dad a kind of power over me.

He was driving, and I was in the passenger's seat. We pulled into the driveway, and he shut off the engine. We sat in awkward silence—as usual. But it finally broke as I chose to speak about my pain. Oddly, I wasn't pointing a finger at him, telling him all the ways he'd failed me. Instead it was a beautiful moment of sharing my perspective of life. God wrapped my words in grace and mercy. I didn't wonder what my dad thought of me. I just wanted him to know who I was, what I felt, what I'd experienced. That day as I spilled the junk in my heart, I let go of the burden of seeking approval from my father.

It's been four years since that conversation. Last month I took my daughter to see my dad. We spent a few days, and it was good—not great, but good. It was what I expected. His words and actions are still much the same. He's a good man who has made his share of poor decisions, many of which have affected my life. My love for him is as great as ever, but the control he once had is gone. Though his actions once shaped me, they no longer matter. All that matters now is how God sees me.

My name is Andy Mylin, and I am not a blockhead.

▶ TRACK THREE: "IN MY EYES"

TRACK THREE: "IN MY EYES"

> If you're looking in my eyes
> What you'll see is a girl with a plea
> With attempts to disguise
> I'm getting closer and closer to throwing in the
> towel
> In my eyes
> You'll see a plethora of insecurities
> Though I try to deny
> You're the only thing on which I can rely
> I know you're helping
> As you're pouring salt on my wounds

One last blow came on the day of my grandma's funeral. The time had come to leave, and good-byes were being exchanged. I still wanted some kind of connection with my dad, but conversation seemed risky. At least a hug needs no words, I reasoned, and I eagerly threw my arms around my father's waist in an attempted bear hug. His massive arms came to rest on my shoulders like a couple of wet noodles. I felt a hesitant pat or two on my back.

I held on for dear life, hoping, wishing, needing him to

hug me back. He chuckled nervously as he said, "All right, Steph. All right." He tried to back out of my embrace as I began to cry.

"Scott, just hold her," I heard my mom discreetly say in a desperate attempt to see her daughter's need for affection met. Still, all he could give me was a quick little squeeze as he backed away altogether, nearly pushing me out of his reach.

Thank God I was returning home to the one great hope I felt I could hold onto. There was a boy named "Chris" who had said the very words I'd longed to hear from my dad: I love you. He said this to me after only two weeks of dating.

"You can't know that after only a few weeks," I told him. Still, I had never had a boy tell me that I was loved. As Chris persisted in professing his love for me, it began to feel safer to let my heart go.

Chris was a year older than me. He was a friend of my big brother and a competitive swimmer. One weekend, after we'd been dating for a while, he returned home with a gold medal. On the casing he had engraved, "To my Steph: I won this for you. I love you."

I was being wooed. We talked on the phone every night until my mom told me it was time to go to bed. Matt helped me set up my first screen name so Chris and I could chat online. It was very romantic.

Heightening the romance was the fact that, after a full month of dating, I had still not allowed Chris to kiss me. In fact it wasn't until a Saturday afternoon walk the weekend before my grandma's funeral that I had allowed Chris to steal a kiss.

Only eight days later I ventured into our basement where I found Matt chatting online. Sensing my presence, Matt suddenly jumped to his feet and turned to me. "Get out of here, Steph!" he yelled. My startled expression—it wasn't like Matt to yell at me—must have softened him. "I don't think you want to read this," he said more gently.

I immediately felt my gut tighten. "I know it's Chris. What is going on?" I insisted. Matt cleared the way and allowed me to chat with Chris myself. And there I sat, using my brother's screen name as I got dumped.

Just in case you have never been a 14-year-old girl, let me break this down for you. When a girl is 14, attention from boys—right or wrong—is very important. To a girl, a boy wanting to be her boyfriend translates into him saying, "I think you are very valuable, and I like you." So you can imagine that when he says, "I think we should just be friends," it translates to, "I find no value in you, and frankly, I no longer like you." This is not what Chris said to me, but in my mind I had just received the second of my double-whammy messages from the two most important guys in my life.

These messages of rejection from my dad and from Chris affixed themselves to my brain like a stubborn piece of already-been-chewed gum to the underside of a school cafeteria table. They were not the only messages I had stored away there. Just like the lies of self-loathing already calcifying in my brain, I found them impossible to get rid of. They played in my mind over and over again: He didn't want you. You didn't meet his standards. He didn't like you. You weren't good enough. You were not his dream.

I cried some and retreated into myself a bit. I even briefly entertained the thought of hurting myself. For some reason God helped me not to travel too far down my self-destructive road just yet.

CHOOSE YOUR PLAYLIST: TRUTH OR CONSEQUENCES?

Depression is an interesting concept, but of course, it's more than a concept. I know it's a very real thing—I have found myself caught in its dizzying, downward spiral. And spiral is a good picture for depression because it's not instantaneous. It creeps up on you. Without even realizing it's happening, you are suddenly immobilized, caught in its grip.

In the weeks after the funeral and the break-up, my grades dropped; I put on weight; I had no interest in anything. My mom thought I had mononucleosis and took me to the doctor. I still remember the doctor emerging with results from the blood test. He had pamphlets in his hand. "Well, it's not mono," he said. "But I'd like to talk with you about clinical depression."

"I'm only 14," I shot back. "Doesn't this happen to people when they're older?" The word *clinical* was frightening to me. There was an immediate sense of shame and a desire to keep this news from ever leaking out. I informed my mom that I was pretty sure I could bounce back from this. Just give me some time.

But Mom was on top of things. As a health professional she knew not to mess around with depression. I was given two very clear options: Medicate or talk to a counselor.

It was an easy decision. "I'll talk," I said.

To be truthful I saw the counselor only four or five times. She helped me understand that my dad's disease alters his personality at times. It wasn't that my dad didn't want to know me. She said I actually had all of the tools I needed to work my way to the truth. She was right.

Going into these counseling sessions, I had a

couple of things figured out even at 14. I knew that:

1. Life is not always easy. Bad things happen to everyone.

2. God is bigger than anything else in my life. He loves me.

I did not know the ins and outs or the nuances of these truths, but I had the general ideas down pretty well. Funny, then, that I should still act surprised and bitter when troubles got in my way.

My counselor reminded me that I didn't have to let my life be defined by the hard parts. She said that if I could learn to look for the goodness around me, I might find a lot more of it than I expected. There's a verse in the Bible that encourages us to shift our gaze and see all the good God is doing in our lives. It says, "Finally, brothers and sisters, whatever is true, whatever is noble, whatever is right, whatever is pure, whatever is lovely, whatever is admirable—if anything is excellent or praiseworthy—think about such things. Whatever you have learned or received or heard from me, or seen in me—put it into practice. And the God of peace will be with you" (Philippians 4:8-9).

I know this lesson may sound simplistic, but the truth is often simple. And often it's right in front of our noses. We miss it because we don't fine-tune our focus. Or we focus on the wrong thing.

At 14 I had been handed a blow that felt like rejection. It would be foolish to believe that a person of any age or maturity level could ignore the hurt. However, my mom and my counselor would not let me focus on that hurt for too long—I would have been swimming upstream against the truth. So instead of only talking about my dad or my past or the pain I was dealing with, my counselor asked me also to talk about other parts of my life. "So what do you like to do?" she'd ask. "Tell me about yourself."

And I told her about art. It was everything to me. I enrolled in every art class my school would allow me to take. Oh yeah, and music. Music helped me feel alive. I didn't tell anyone I wanted to be a rock star—that whole fear of failure thing or maybe fear of being laughed at. But I chose to confide in my counselor.

"Did you know that when Stephanie talks about music she just lights up?" my counselor asked my mom. "It's like someone flips a switch in her."

I'm not sure why, but a month after I started seeing my counselor, I found myself struggling again. I think there was a lure to playing the victim. I could have a little pity party and get some attention. But it wasn't just that. I was truly feeling the heaviness of rejection again. One night at youth group, my pastor, Jonathan, was dismissing everyone. Just as we were on our way out the door, he suddenly slammed on the brakes.

"Everyone stop! I think we need to pray against the spirit of depression."

I hit my seat and was instantaneously broken. *I haven't told anyone about this! How does he know? What should I say?* But I was learning that sickness depends on secrets. If I really wanted to recover, I had to be honest. It was time to get real with my friends.

 ## Your song

Here's the deal. If you're holding on to secret pain in hopes that everyone will think you're doing just fine, I've got news for you: You're not really fooling anyone. People see it in your eyes. But until you can bring yourself to get real with the people in your life, your "secret" is going to keep eating away at you. You have to tell someone. The first few words will be the hardest, but it will get better after that.

If your secret is depression, then I have more news for you: You're not alone, not by a long shot. Though it's nearly impossible to measure accurately, the National Institute of Mental Health estimates that approximately 20.9 million people in America are struggling with depression of some sort. And that's just the people who are talking about it.

Maybe you're not sure if the darkness inside you is depression. It's important to know what depression is—and isn't. There is depression, and then there's sadness. Everyone feels sad now and then, particularly when reeling from any number of hurtful experiences this life can dish out. This normal grieving tends to lessen as time goes by. But depression doesn't lessen. It doesn't fade. It just gets deeper and darker. And while depression is common, it's not normal. It's not the way we are supposed to feel. It's not something you need to live with. You can get better.

If you or someone you know has been exhibiting signs of depression for more than two weeks—loss of appetite, loss of sleep or unusual amounts of sleep, disinterest in activities that were once favorites, feelings of wanting to hurt yourself, emotional numbness—it's time to talk to a professional. Start by talking to your pastor or another Christian you trust. Ask that person to help you find a Christian counselor. It is of utmost importance that counseling be based on the foundation of God's Word—your faith plays an enormous role in how you deal with depression. Other excellent organizations, such as New Life Ministries (www.newlife.com or 1-800-NEW-LIFE), can offer recommendations for a qualified counselor in your area.

SO YOU WANT TO BE A ROCK STAR?

Beating Depression
by Chris S. Heinz

When I was in college, I checked into a mental hospital. This is not what I planned to do my senior year, but in the end, I'm glad I did. My official condition was clinical depression, although on the surface it didn't seem as if I had anything to be depressed about. I had a lot going for me—more than others had, you might have thought.

I came from a loving upper-middle-class family. We went to church every week. In high school I was active in youth group. During the summers I went to a Christian sports camp where I won an award for godliness and later worked as a camp counselor. I was selected for *Who's Who Among American High School Students* multiple times and was an Academic All-American. I chose to attend a Christian college where I became known for a strong faith. I was a Bible study leader, dorm resident assistant, and Bible major. I looked as if I had it all together.

But then the world turned dark. I don't know the specific moment that the depression started, but it took over pretty quickly. Normally warm and outgoing, I became cold and detached. I shut my shades and stayed in my room as much as possible. I started smoking cigarettes and stashed alcohol in my closet so I could drink in my room. And thoughts of suicide filled my mind every day. I would imagine different ways of killing myself.

I wanted to look put together. I didn't want to disappoint the people around me. I mean, there were people in the world living in far worse conditions, so what excuse did I have for all this mess? No, I resolved to put on a happy face in public. I forced myself to leave my room, go to class, and socialize. I only smoked at home, so the only people who knew about it were my housemates. And I was convinced that for the most part, my life looked the way it always had.

My breaking point came one night when I was watching a movie alone in the house. In the movie the main character was dying in a hospital bed. Friends and neighbors—practically the whole town—came to pay their last respects. Suddenly the thought pierced my mind: *I wonder if anyone would visit me if I were dying.* Then as quickly as the question was asked, it was answered: *Of course not. You're not worth it.* That answer confirmed what I suspected all along.

I crumbled to the ground in a heap, tears streaming down my face, my chest heaving in deep sobs. I clawed at the hardwood floor with my fingernails and kicked the ground with my feet. I butted my head against the ground. At that moment I believed no one would come to my deathbed, that I wasn't worth the effort. I believed that all the God-talk I had heard my whole life was just that—talk. *I believed* I was nothing and I needed to die.

My mind turned to my parents. I knew that my death would tear them apart. And I didn't want to do that to my family. So I called home. When my parents answered I couldn't even speak. I cried and cried and cried, and I could hear them crying with me. They told me they'd find extended care for me, and I agreed to go wherever they wanted me to go.

A few days later they picked me up, and we drove to an out-of-state hospital with an excellent mental health program. My parents said good-bye to me at the hospital right before the nurse locked me in. I know now that it was one of the most difficult moments of their lives. As they drove away, my parents wondered, *Where did things go so wrong? How did we come to this?* I wondered the same thing.

My time in the hospital wasn't pleasant. It was filled with dark moments. One night I pressed a lit cigarette into the palm of my hand. I wanted to feel the intensity of the pain. I wanted my body to hurt. The cigarette left a small, round scar in the middle of my palm. But in the midst of this anguish, I began to see glimmers of light, bits of hope that I might actually move through this and come out okay. And that's what happened.

Through my therapy, I came to see that my depression came on in part because I didn't know who I was. I didn't know where my value came from. I'd always been an achiever, always excelled at nearly everything I did. And it wasn't enough. I didn't know how to find peace with myself or how to find value in who I was. I could only look for that peace, that sense of worth, through the things I did. But it wasn't there.

The whole mess—my depression, its cover-up, the secret drinking, the dark, dark nights, the desperation—all of it hinged on figuring out who I was. And finding my identity saved me.

Here's what it is: I am who God says I am. It's that simple. I've found that my biggest battles in life—the ones where I fight with myself or others or spiritual forces—are won when I remember this statement: I am who God says I am. I don't have to try to be someone I'm not. I don't have to prove my worth to other people by being cool or tough or perfect. And I don't have to listen to the voice of the enemy that tries to tell me I'm not worthy of love.

The challenge is to listen and believe what God says about me. It's not always easy because most of the time this stuff sounds unbelievable: I am a child of God. I am created in the image of God. I am beloved by God. I am worthy of God's love. I have been saved from my doubt and shame and insecurity by the love of God. I will live with God forever.

But I figure this is God we're talking about, so it's okay if it sounds unbelievable. Because there is no love like God's love. There is no peace like God's peace. There is no future like God's future. God surpasses all human understanding. And when I remember that, I actually believe that I am who God says I am.

There are many voices out there trying to tell me that God is wrong about me. But the scar on my left hand is a reminder that those voices only lead to more pain. I used to pray the scar would go away. But it hasn't. Now I hope it doesn't. I look down and am reminded to stay close to God's voice. Because I am who he says I am.

TRACK FOUR: "BEAUTY"

> Cause I like who I am underneath
>
> and there is so much more to me
>
> than what you see...
>
> Beauty is in you, you don't have to make it
>
> You don't have to fake it
>
> Beauty is in you, so just embrace it
>
> You don't have to chase it

I don't know how this happened. You may have a hard time believing me, but I arrived at my 15th year somehow having been sheltered from the media's view of beauty. I was not a small girl—always tall and at the top of the growth charts if you get my drift. Still I repeatedly looked into mirrors and thought I was seeing what everyone would define as true beauty.

A guy in my math class named Eric was giving me every reason to believe he saw the same thing. Valentine's Day, the day of harbored teenage insecurities, was getting closer and closer. I was by no means what one would call a smooth talker, but I had carefully observed my girlfriends in their attempts to master the art of flirtation. So when Eric made a regular effort to sit next to me in fifth period algebra, I thought it right to at least put my best foot forward. After all it was only in response to his first move.

I tried to not get my hopes up. I wouldn't let myself believe there was anything more than a blossoming friendship between us. But there was a part of me that desired from Eric the affirmation that I was lovely and mysterious and worth a second look. A squealing phone call from my friend D'Anne confirmed the fact that he was indeed planning to ask me to the Valentine's Day Dance. "He said he is going to ask you. He's gonna ask, Steph."

But when the day of the dance arrived with still no invite, I was on the verge of panic. To make matters their absolute worst, Eric didn't show up in math class that day.

"Where's Eric?" I whispered anxiously to D'Anne as class wrapped up.

"Don't worry about it. Wait, do we have any homework tonight?"

"D'Anne?!" I growled in a whisper.

"What? I don't know, okay?"

"D'Anne, what's going on? Did you talk to him at all? He hasn't asked me yet, you know."

She continued to pack her books as if she had somewhere important to go and shook her head as she encouraged me to just let it go. I followed her out of the classroom, down the hall, and to our lockers. She busied herself at her locker and gave herself a look in the little magnetic locker mirror. "D, please, what are you not telling me?"

"Fine, Steph," she said. "I don't want to tell you; I don't. It's awful, but because you insist. He said he decided not to ask you because he thinks you're chunky...and annoying."

"What? I am not." I initially responded, but as the sting of those words sunk in, the tears started. Not only had he attacked my appearance, but my personality. What did I have to fall back on? I found my way to the restroom around the corner with D'Anne following. As I looked in the mirror, it was as though blinders were removed from my eyes. What before had never caused me grief to look at now disgusted me.

It was just one comment from a boy who doesn't mean anything to me today, but I likely will never forget his assessment of me. I was lacking both personality and physique. I wasn't quite sure what to do with my annoying self, but the question of my largeness was much easier to deal with.

Home was not an inviting place at the time. Mom was always working. Matt was in sports every day after school. And we had taken in a friend of Matt's who was going through a hard time of her own with depression. I began to enjoy taking long walks every evening after school to escape—it significantly accelerated my weight loss. Other people took notice, too. It was so empowering. There was one specific Wednesday I remember contemplating my new shape. It was better, but it wasn't enough. I wanted more weight loss. I wanted more of this power I was feeling. And the solution was simple: If I stop eating, I will lose weight much faster.

I went to youth group that night, and Jonathan, my youth pastor, plopped down next to me. "How you doing?" he asked.

"I'm good." Thin. A little smile. More secrets.

"I want to tell you something," he said. He turned his face away from me as if he were trying hard to recall exactly what he wanted to say. "I don't even know what this means—but I was doing my devos this morning, and God showed up and said *Stephanie is beautiful.* I was like, Yeah, God, we all know that. But then he said it again. *Stephanie is beautiful.*

He wasn't even looking at me—it was a typical Jonathan-talks-to-the-wind moment. Then suddenly he turned to me and said, "Does that mean anything to y—Whoa! I guess it does."

I was sobbing.

CHOOSE YOUR PLAYLIST: PRINCESS OR UGLY DUCKLING?

When I talk to young girls, I often tell them about that day in youth group. "Is it a secret to you that I'm tall?" I ask the girls. (I won't be in the WNBA any time soon, but I do top out at 5'9" feet.) What might be a secret is that I've been this tall since eighth grade. Honestly I've never been very comfortable with my height. I always stuck out. I was even taller than my older brother for 13 years. His friends called me Truck because I could tackle him.

It wasn't until much later that I began to learn that I was holding onto a pattern of "stinkin' thinkin'" in regard to my beauty. And here's why it's stinkin'.

I have always believed the Word of God to be true. And the Bible says that God made everything. Looking at everything God has created, I have no choice but to praise him: *You are flawless, God. All that you have created is wonderful and without comparison...except me. I think you were supposed to make me shorter...thinner...faster...you* fill in the blank.

What a contradiction to praise God as perfect, to see God's hand in all of creation, then to say, "But you messed up on me. You made a mistake." That's contrary to the God I know, love, and worship. And as we talk about choices, it strikes me that there are choices here: The choice to start wisely eating the good food God made. The choice to stop forcing yourself to vomit, purging away the calories you piled on in hopes you wouldn't feel so awful. The choice to stop eating too much. The choice to be honest about how you feel about yourself. The choice to love yourself.

But you can't make those choices without first making far more basic choices: Will I believe God when he says that he created me in love, that he made me beautiful and wonderful and just as I should be? Or will I believe that I know better, that I can remake myself to be everything God neglected to make me?

We need to understand something about this God we serve. He is very intentional. Do you realize the miracles that take place in your body every single day? Our outer features are wonderful—we'll get to those in a moment—but do you realize the forethought your Creator gave to your inner workings?

The average human body contains about six quarts of blood, which are pumped through your heart about once every minute. That means your heart is pumping more than 1,500 gallons of blood every day. Your liver carefully measures every component in that blood, intercepting any toxic substances and breaking them down so that the rest of the organs can function normally. The kidneys miraculously know exactly what balance of alkaline and acid your blood needs and make adjustments you don't even feel in order to achieve that balance. And, of course, I haven't even mentioned the brain—a human computer responsible for every movement, memory, emotion, and idea you have ever produced.

Great care was taken to create your beauty as well. Take your hair, for example. Our hairs, roughly 100,000 of them on our heads, grow from tiny "pits" in the skin called follicles. Neither *pit* nor *follicle* is a pretty word, but this is cool nonetheless. Near each follicle on your entire body God placed a sebaceous gland, which periodically secretes a kind of oil into the follicle in order to keep your hair soft and manageable, as the TV commercials would say. Now that's forethought.

Here is a statement about your miraculous eyes that may cause you to scratch your head, unless you are a biologist: Each human eye possesses 120 million light-sensitive rods and 7 million cones that convert light into chemical impulses. Charles Darwin freely admitted that the eye was one piece of human anatomy he found difficult to reconcile with his theory of natural selection. (Of course, he tried anyway.) "To suppose," Darwin admitted, "that the eye with all its inimitable contrivances...could have been formed by natural selection, seems, I freely confess, absurd in the highest degree" (Darwin, 167). God created the eye not only to take in his beauty but to be beautiful in its own right.

You are a spectacular, magnificently planned, highly detailed creation. And once you realize this, that little beauty-demon will never get in your head again, right? Well, unfortunately, no. It still gets me sometimes. But I've given God permission to get into the dialogue with me these days.

"I wish my butt were smaller."

Hey, I put some thought into that butt, okay?

And God's right. Even if I were a marathon runner, I'd probably still have a curvy butt. I was created intentionally. Crafted, not thrown together. If I could give one gift to every girl everywhere, it would be this belief—You were created by a God who is intentional in all things, even in the way he made you.

Your song

Here's a challenge for you. Let's take a beauty fast.

Choose one aspect of your beauty regimen—your eye makeup, your zit cover-up, your diet, the two-hour shampoo and straightening iron marathons—and lay it aside for a week. If we have to check something in the mirror (or on the scale) every time we pass, there is an imbalance in our lives.

Instead, breathe this prayer to God: Creator God, I stand again at a crossroads where I need to choose. Will I believe today that you intentionally crafted me and that your love for me is unquenchable? Help my unbelief. Amen.

SO YOU WANT TO BE A ROCK STAR?

Life after a Major Injury
by Alison Rose

Life seemed perfect back in 2001. I was serving God with Campus Crusade for Christ at the University of Michigan, growing closer to the Lord, telling others about Jesus, hanging out with great friends, and simply basking in all God was doing in my life. That suddenly changed on a dusky evening in Newport Beach, California.

While playing in the ocean with some Campus Crusade students, I dove through a wave that seemed to body-slam me to the ocean floor, causing me to break my neck. I instantly was paralyzed from the chest down. The students pulled me out of the water and onto the shore. I was in a hospital bed before my hair had even dried.

Initially the doctors were hopeful that the damaged nerves in my spinal cord would heal and bring back movement. But as time went on, that hope began to fade. I spent the next six months in rehab, relearning how to feed myself, get dressed, put on makeup, strengthen my arms, transfer from my bed to my wheelchair, and more. It was a long, hard road. I was confused as to what God was doing. I believed him to be good, yet wondered why this was happening.

I wrestled with questions such as "What now?" "How can this be better?" "How can I do this?" And even still, on my hardest days, I continue to wrestle with those same questions. Yet in the midst of it all, I have been hopeful that maybe God chose me for something greater. In those first awful months, I sensed God was there. I sensed God gently saying, *Okay?* and I found myself peacefully responding, *Okay.* I've seen God provide for me and bless me in ways I would never trade for the full use of my body. I've seen God use me to help others who are hurting and those who have lost hope in the goodness of God. He really is faithful.

I hold on to 1 Corinthians 13:12-13, which says, "Now we see only a reflection as in a mirror; then we shall see face to face. Now I know in part; then I shall know fully, even as I am fully known. And now these three remain: faith, hope and love. But the greatest of these is love." We don't always know now why God allows pain and suffering, but one day we will. Until then we can have faith in God's promise to be with us in the midst of our pain. We can hold on to the hope of heaven, where there will be no more tears, where we will love and be loved forever.

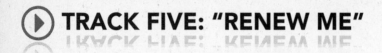

▶ TRACK FIVE: "RENEW ME"

TRACK FIVE: "RENEW ME"

> Another day, and before I begin
>
> Something within me says
>
> I'm not okay, let's address this emptiness
>
> Cause I'm really a mess
>
> Savior of this heart
>
> You renew me
>
> And let me start again

Heading off to college a few years later, I decided it was time to pursue my call in life—or what I thought was my call—to be a rock star. And that's exactly what I did. I pursued.

If you know anything about callings, a red flag should be going up about now. A calling isn't something we make happen. It's something that God extends to us. And yet as I set out to establish my identity as a person of renown, there was a lot of misplaced striving on my behalf. I was willing to do whatever I thought I had to do to make a name for myself. As a result, I spent the first six months of my college life being an idiot.

It didn't take long for an opportunity to arise, and I immediately assumed it was a sign of God's hand at work. I was invited to be the lead singer for a promising band made up of my fellow students at Greenville College in Illinois. It convinced me that being in a band was the call God had on my life. The problem here between God and me? I didn't take time to listen—or even to ask for that matter. These guys were older, fame hungry like I was, and had all been in bands before. I didn't know them well and never bothered to ask any questions. They stood on the stage with me, and I chose to believe they had it together.

But we didn't have it together. None of us. By the end of our first six months together, some things started to come out, and I'm talking about some pretty serious issues. I knew this gig was quickly unraveling from all sides, but I closed my eyes tighter and chanted the same useless mantras over and over.

I just need to be a good example.

I can help them.

No one else needs to know.

But I swear this is the calling in my life!

On the music front we really thought this was

it. We had regular shows, a short tour, label interest. But on the personal front, I had worked my way into an impossible situation. It had become clear that one of my married bandmates had feelings for me. There I was at 19 trying to counsel two people through the shrapnel of a failing marriage—a counseling gig I had absolutely no business conducting. After all, much of that shrapnel involved me.

Wouldn't you know it was Mom to the rescue again? She called one night and said, "Steph, I feel an urgency for you to take care of this situation. Today. Now. You need to sit those two down and tell them you are out. They cannot call you any longer. They cannot confide in you or seek your counsel. Do it now, Steph." She also told me, "Be sure you take a witness with you."

The next day the band kicked "Jim" out. I was gone a week later, but steeled by the wisdom of my mom and the support of my friend Ryan who had been my witness through this intervention of sorts.

Though God had been working in my life and I had turned a corner, I knew I was in a bad place. I had been someone ugly. I was not proud of it. My mom had said to me earlier that summer, "I don't like who you are, and I don't care if this band is taken away from you." And now, as much as I wanted to convince everyone that I was a new person, that God had decimated those unquenchable desires for fame and attention, I realized my words had no real credibility any longer. The midnight hour found me crying an absolute river of brokenness, repentance, and confession on a spare bed at my mentor's house.

I confessed it all to this woman who had become my safe place. She was the mother of one of my classmates. In my quest for attention and affirmation from the world, I was sure that I had alienated everyone else, yet Cindy had remained a steady source of grace in my life. Now I needed some mercy. There is a line that every "good girl" fears to cross. Though I could honestly say I had never set foot on the other side of that line, there was no way I could hide the fact that I had been doing some serious cozying up to it. Doing so broke up a band. It flatlined a marriage. And by this time I knew without a doubt that it had broken God's heart.

I felt God invite me right then and there to rebuild everything in my life. We were going to start from square one.

 ## CHOOSE YOUR PLAYLIST: SERVANT OR ROCK STAR?

God has a plan for you, all right. Have you ever wondered what that plan is? It's pretty straightforward, though the Bible lays it out in a variety of ways. Here are a few clear examples of God's will for our lives:

"Religion that God our Father accepts as pure and faultless is this: to look after orphans and widows in their distress and to keep oneself from being polluted by the world." (James 1:27)

"He has shown all you people what is good. And what does the LORD require of you? To act justly and to love mercy and to walk humbly with your God." (Micah 6:8)

"Therefore go and make disciples of all nations, baptizing them in the name of the Father and of the Son and of the Holy Spirit." (Matthew 28:19)

Do you see the common thread in those verses? We complicate this notion of God's will for our lives. We think God has secret little plans just for us that we have to find. And if we don't find them, we'll have wasted our lives or missed the chance to do what God wanted us to do. We get so focused on trying to find God's will that when we finally come up for a panicked breath, we look around only to find we've left God in our dust.

God's will is the same for all of us. He's made it fairly simple—he had to for people like me. God wants you to love him with your whole heart and with all your strength. God wants you to love other people. God wants you to live your life in such a way that other people see God in you.

When you read the previous verses, it's easy to see how a rock star could do those things. But it's also easy to see that there's absolutely nothing in any of those verses that would tolerate a rock star, look-at-me attitude.

Believe it or not, each of us is led to the crossroads of fame at some point in our life. It's the crossroads that begs this question: Who gets the glory? Is it me? Or is it God? It is the crossroads of rebellion and humility. Which road will we take?

This is the same question Satan once had to wrestle with, the one that brought him to his crossroads of rebellion. Of course you know the outcome of the story, but do you know the beginning? Satan actually was once an angel, given life even before the creation of the earth. You've probably heard him referred to in Sunday school as a fallen angel. There is a lot of debate centered on a passage in Ezekiel (28:12-17), which at first glance seems to be describing Satan. It says he was the model of perfection, full of wisdom and perfect in beauty. He was dressed in an array of precious stones that had been prepared specifically for him. Many Bible scholars convincingly argue that this passage is not about Satan, but about the King of Tyre, who was filled with such promise in his early reign yet fell prey to temptations caused by fame, power, and money. His pride absolutely decimated him.

Either way, it applies to my story, doesn't it? The quest for fame—or even just getting noticed— is a natural desire for human beings. But there is such an inherent danger in that quest. I was willing to compromise who I was and what I believed to make it with this band. I never dreamed I would cave on those things, but I did. The sin of pride, my need to be noticed and to be important took over. But when we seek God's help, God in his mercy doesn't leave us mired in that sin. He makes a way for us to come back to him again and again if we so choose.

The thing that strikes me about our rebellion is that God is such a gentleman about the whole thing. Romans 14:11 makes it quite clear there will come a day when every knee on earth will bow to him. His commandments make it pretty clear, as well, that there is no room for any God other than him. But, oh, the grace he gives us as we wrestle with the decision of whether we will let God be in control.

By the time I was beginning to figure all of

this out, my life had taken quite a dramatic turn. I ran away—from school, from fame, from music. But I ran straight into the arms of a loving God who wanted to teach me about his true will for my life: his good, pleasing, and perfect will. It wasn't a rock star he needed after all.

Your song

Movie night with friends! Get a group together and watch one of the following flicks. Then take some time to discuss fame, humility, and God's will for our lives.

For the artsy crowd: *Waiting for Guffman*

For the athlete: *Rudy*

For the musician: *That Thing You Do*

For the budding theologian: *The Mission*

For the dancer: *Fame* or *A Chorus Line*

For the aspiring politician: *Dave*

For a silly night: *Evan Almighty*

SO YOU WANT TO BE A ROCK STAR?

When God Gives You a Do-Over
by Rachel Thomas

I grew up filled with mixed emotions. I have a bi-racial background—my biological father is black, and my mother is white. They divorced when I was three years old. To this day, I don't know why. I grew up with my mom and stepfather. My stepfather, who is white, seemed to think my existence was something to be mocked, and he was very good at hurting my siblings and me with racist comments. It didn't take me long to develop a kind of identity crisis. I just didn't fit in anywhere, not with any race, not with any crowd at school, not even in my own family. And I desperately wanted to fit in.

In eighth grade I finally found the keys to popularity and happiness, or so I thought. That year I tried marijuana for the first time. At the age of 15, I lost my virginity. It all left me feeling ashamed, humiliated, and scared. In the back of my mind, I wondered *What is my worth? Do I have any value? Why do I even exist?* I was on a fast road to self-destruction.

I didn't see it that way, of course. I was too numb. I started drinking alcohol. I did cocaine a few times. I even tried ecstasy once. I would go to parties dressed in revealing clothes; my "friends" would tell me how cute I looked and how well I danced. I thought I was a rock star. But I had this little voice of shame inside me, too. I remember, in the midst of it all, saying to God, "If you are there, God, I'm sorry."

During my junior year of high school, I started dating a guy named Josh. I became pregnant with my first child the last month of my senior year. This is exactly what I did not want to happen. Josh stayed with me, and we tried to make some kind of life together. But we fought all the time. One huge fight sent me to jail overnight; it was the worst place to be. I cried the entire time.

Eventually Josh and I got married, but soon we were broke, unhappy, and living with my mom. That was a disaster. My mom and I fought. My mom and Josh fought. Josh and I fought. One day my mom got so upset with me that she tried to strangle me. I was too afraid to move, so I just stood there and took it. When she finally let go, Josh and I packed our stuff and left.

We moved in with Josh's parents. We were like a couple of ill-mannered cats clawing at each other all the time. At one point Josh's parents kicked me out of the house. I spent three days at a women's shelter with my one-year-old child and the second one on the way. I felt completely alone. I remember thinking, *What did I do wrong? I am not perfect, but why is this all happening to me? Why can't anybody just love me?* I was as lonely as I'd ever been.

Then something happened. Josh came to get me at the shelter. I had expected him to leave me there, to get out of our bad marriage, and to find someone better. But he didn't. He chose me; he chose our children; he chose to try again. And that's what we did.

We moved to Pennsylvania and started to attend church. We really tried to work things out, but we didn't know how. The people at the church loved us and cared about us, but we still couldn't break out of our old patterns of anger and pain. I was determined that I would have a life full of joy. I had seen enough sorrow and hatred. I just wanted peace in my heart and in my home.

I knew that whatever needed to change wasn't on the outside. The thing that needed fixing was inside me. I asked my pastor what I needed to do to change my life. He and his wife came to my house, talked with me for a long time, then asked if I wanted to have Jesus in my heart. "Yes!" I shouted. That was July 4, 2002, and nothing has been the same since. The old Rachel died that day, and a new Rachel was raised up through the love of Jesus Christ.

God reminds me all the time that he is the Father of the fatherless. He is the only way, the only truth, the only life I need. God reminds me that he knew me before I said yes to life with him. He chose me. The old life is gone, and the new life is here. I was broken and empty, but God is shaping me into who I was supposed to be from the beginning of time. He loves me. I am his, and he is mine. Nothing can separate me from the love he has for me. God says he delights in me. When I am ugly he says I am lovely. When the enemy brings up the past, I don't listen. I tell him what God says.

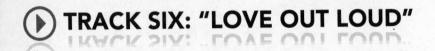

TRACK SIX: "LOVE OUT LOUD"

It's time, I got something to say

Cause every time I turn around

I'm hearing love, but it ain't loud

We gotta turn it up now

And what I mean is words are more than cheap

Lip service is a waste of time

I'm tired of talking,

You and I could start a revolution

I didn't even make it out of the airport. I had gone to Guatemala in an effort to get some clarity in my life. Yes, I was running away from all the shame of the past year, but I just couldn't move forward without some serious time alone with God. So when the opportunity came to head to Guatemala for a few months, I took it.

As soon as I landed back in the United States, I called my mom. That's when I learned there was no money for school the next semester.

"Listen, Steph," my mom said, "I've been trying to

get ahold of you for the past few days. You have to take care of this. You either need to call your dad and ask him for the money, or you need to move home."

My dad. My dad whom I had not seen or spoken to since the funeral? I called him the next day and started crying as soon as he answered the phone.

I really didn't know what to call him. "S... Scott?" I stuttered.

"Yeah?"

"This is Stephanie."

"Who?" *Aaagh. Not this again.*

"Stephanie—your daughter." At this point I went on an incoherent rant that ranged from South America to my bankbook to my little school in Illinois.

"Well, slow down now. I can't understand you." I remember him being very gentle. Man, his southern drawl was deep.

I was finally able to explain to him my need for money, and he asked me to give him a day to look into things. I wasn't sure if I'd hear from him again, but the next day he called to let me know he had everything set up for me. I was going to be able to continue school. And then my dad gave me his first priceless daddy-daughter gift.

I could tell it was hard for him to say it. But I could also tell he was sincere. "Listen, Stephanie, it was so good to hear from you, and I've been thinking I'd really like to see you."

Wow. All this time he didn't know where I was. But as we talked he realized that we'd been closer than he'd ever imagined. My dad was a truck driver, and his route took him within miles of my college nearly every week.

"How about next Thursday?" he asked.

The day I was going to meet my dad, I sat in anthropology class with my stomach doing flip-flops. Five years had passed since the funeral, but this time I knew we'd recognize each other right away. As I walked through the doors of the truck stop, I spotted him sitting alone in a booth. He looked as white as a ghost. Scared. Innocent. My heart immediately went out to him. I knew he was trying so hard, and this was really a stretch for him.

He ordered a salad with ranch dressing—the dressing kept dripping down his chin, which melted my heart all the more. I found him mesmerizing and felt for the first time a deep and unexplainable love birthed in my heart. We looked at pictures of Guatemala, and I told him about college. He was in awe. "Well, I can't believe this. You turned out all right," he said. He gave me $100 and told me to take care of my car.

A week or two passed, and I was *still* hearing from him—one time he called and said, "I just wanted to hear your voice. This is so cool. Gosh, this is so cool."

Then a letter unexpectedly arrived in the mail. As I read it I felt like I had just taken a big punch to the solar plexus.

"Dear Steph,

I thought I could do this, but I was wrong. Let's face it. The best years of your life were taken from me, and I'm too old and messed up to try now. So from now on please pretend I am dead. I will see you in Heaven.

—Your loser dad."

I kid you not, God showed up then and there and said, *Okay, Steph, you have a choice. You can put on another wound, or you can lay that at my feet. You can continue walking in the love I've been showing you, or you can play the victim.*

CHOOSE YOUR PLAYLIST: BETTER OR BITTER?

On one hand we could focus from this point forward on how no 13-, 19-, 24-, or 50-year-old should ever have to bear the weight of estrangement from a parent. We could run through the findings of another statistical study to prove that we are far from alone. But you and I both know this world was damaged upon delivery—our delivery into the world, that is. And I hope that by now you also realize there is no such thing as a perfect family.

When it comes to relationships in this world, I believe God has asked us to improvise in a way. Here's what I mean. Think right now of a relationship that fits into each of the following categories and place that person's name in the blank.

One of my best friends is _____.

A parent I'm in relationship with is _____.

A leader or mentor in ministry I know the best is _____.

Now, is it at all possible that any of the three relationships above are without fault? Can you tell me that you have gone unhurt by any of the three? Can you guarantee that all three will be in your life five years from now? What life-altering events will these people have to go through in the near future, and how will that impact your relationship?

God knows the answers to these questions, but you and I do not. We will have to wait and see what the next year, five years, or 15 years will bring to our relationships. In the meantime we have to improvise—figure out how to nurture these relationships even when they don't go the way we wish they would. To do that, we need grace, compassion, patience, and humility. After all, there will be times when we are the ones making a relationship difficult.

The relationships we have with other human beings are exceedingly fragile. They are precious and worthy of great care. But they will often disappoint us. We must accept that life—particularly life with other people—ebbs and flows around us.

There is a time for everything,

and a season for every activity under the heavens:

a time to be born and a time to die,

a time to plant and a time to uproot,

a time to kill and a time to heal,

a time to tear down and a time to build,

a time to weep and a time to laugh,

a time to mourn and a time to dance,

a time to scatter stones and a time to gather them,

a time to embrace and a time to refrain,

a time to search and a time to give up,

a time to keep and a time to throw away,

a time to tear and a time to mend,

a time to be silent and a time to speak,

a time to love and a time to hate,

a time for war and a time for peace.

(Ecclesiastes 3:1-8)

How is that for some great songwriting? Life does indeed go in cycles. Turn, turn, turn. Matthew Henry has been dead for a long time—since 1714 to be exact. Yet even before the birth of the United States, before World Wars I and II, and before hip-hop music and the Internet, Presbyterian minister Matthew Henry said this about Ecclesiastes 3—and I suppose about this world we call home today: "To expect *unchanging happiness* in a changing world, must end in disappointment. To bring ourselves to our state in life, is our *duty and wisdom* in this world. *God's whole plan* for the government of the world will be found altogether wise, just, and good. Then let us seize the favourable opportunity for *every good purpose and work*" (htmlbible.com, emphasis added).

That's pretty good advice. Let's break it down a little bit and let this wisdom achieve its full effect.

Unchanging happiness: If you expect always to be happy, disappointment is certain to come your way. Happiness cannot be one of our building blocks for life. Thank God we have happy moments nearly every day! But happiness is an emotion that comes and goes. It is entirely circumstantial.

Think about this. You arrive at Cedar Point, the Roller Coaster Capital of the World, in Sandusky, Ohio, with a group of your friends. The sun is shining, glistening on the surface of Lake Erie. It's a

Wednesday, and the park isn't packed at all. You feel ecstatic. Two rides into the day you suddenly realize that the $60 cash once tucked securely in your back pocket was not secure after all. It is gone. Who knows when it left? You have already made your way to a far corner of the park—for all you know, you lost it back near the entrance. Right. As if the person who finds it will actually come looking for you. Still, you have to look for it. You find one faithful friend who is willing to throw away a good chunk of her day, and you begin the unhappy trek of retracing your steps back to the main gate. Is the entire day a wash? Not necessarily. A 100-mph roller coaster can probably see to it that a state of happiness is reborn, even if the money never resurfaces. Money is not eternal, after all. But neither is happiness. You see, circumstances change for the average person dozens of times per day.

Duty and wisdom: There is a certain task God has given to every one of us. We are expected to move toward maturity in Christ. Everyone has had to do this. Joseph had to rise above abusive brothers, slavery, and prison. Peter had to hold his head up again after three times denying that he knew Jesus. Corrie Ten Boom had to look into the eyes of one of her Nazi captors and offer forgiveness. Sometimes we look at one another with disdain and offer the common insult, "Oh, grow up!" This is actually a perversion of the very nudge we receive from Jesus. Peter says to crave pure spiritual milk so that we can grow up into our salvation (1 Peter 2:2). Only a little child insists on happiness and her own way all the time—okay, some adults do, too. When we grow up we need to realize that not every cloud is going to give us that long-awaited snow day—sometimes it's just going to dump some nasty sleet.

God's whole plan: This is where some faith is required. You and I make plans all the time. We have to, or we would never achieve anything. We plan simple things, such as what to have for dinner tonight. We ponder the significant, such as what to study in college, which job to take, or whom to marry. But we also have to figure out if we believe a couple of things that the Bible says.

"Many are the plans in a human heart, but it is the LORD's purpose that prevails" (Proverbs 19:21). You can make all the plans you want, but if God in his providence wants to change those plans—well, guess whose plans are going to happen? We can fight God, but ultimately, what God ordains will come to pass. Do you believe that?

"And we know that in all things God works for the good of those who love him, who have been called according to his purpose" (Romans 8:28). When I was faced with that letter from my dad, I had to decide I believed this one. I had one of those, "Really, God? Even this?" conversations with God.

But then I remembered something I felt God telling me when I left my first band: *I have something bet-*

ter for you. At the time I thought that meant there was something better for me than music. In fact, I was out of the music scene for a long time. And when that letter came and I asked my heavenly Father how he was going to deal with this very fresh wound, I felt it again: *I have something better for you.* God wanted me to see that even in my pain he was going to work a miracle of love.

Every good purpose and work: My choice as I looked at my dad's letter was clear. The last time he'd rejected me, it took me years to recover. But my foundation was no longer built on a fragile man's love. This time around I had built my hope on Jesus, and just as he promised, there was a better way. I sat down and wrote my dad an e-mail.

"Dad, if what you wrote is the best way I can love you right now, then so be it. I'll love you from a distance. But I do need you to know that I love you. It's not conditional on you being in my life. I'll be praying for you.

Love, your daughter, Stephanie"

Your song

That term *unconditional* is an important one when it comes to relationships. It's a pretty straightforward concept. Yet few of us know how to approach the people in our lives without conditions. If you're anything like nearly every other human being on the planet, then you have created conditions somewhere in your relationships in either an attempt to protect yourself or to punish someone who has wounded you. In the spirit of honest confession, I can tell you that I have those conditions in my relationships. Because I'm human, too.

So what do those conditions look like in real life?

I will only show my parents affection in private where they can't embarrass me.

I will only stay in this marriage as long as we can live near my family because I am afraid not to have them near.

I am only going to trust you as a friend again if you give me your password so I know what you are saying online about me. You already showed me you can't be trusted.

I'll date you, but I want my own space and my own friends on campus. Don't call me; I'll call you.

I forgive you, but you can't possibly expect me not to tell the story any more. It really hurt my feelings.

Unconditional. What does that look like for you? For me it meant drawing up a game plan. I was going to pray for my dad. I would pray, too, that our relationship would be restored. I didn't want to be stuck in that pain day in and day out, so I decided to look outside my little college world for ways I could pour my life into others. Eventually that search would take me all the way to Africa (more on that later). And most of all I chose to be-lieve God at his word. He said he would cause the pain of this relationship to work for good. *I have better for you*, God said.

There were two coats I could put on as I stepped into this plan: God's "better" or my own coat, the one named "bitter." Which coat are you going to wear?

Take out a journal and begin to evaluate some of your key relationships. Which relationships seem the healthiest right now? What factors are making these re-lationships healthy? Would you attribute these factors to yourself or to the other person? Do the same for your most fragile relationships. What is causing them to be unhealthy? Is this due to you or to the other person? In each relationship see if there is one expectation or condition you can "remove" from the other person. Con-tinue to journal for a few months, and see if your "coat" changes. And here's a hint—look for the changes not as much in others as in you.

SO YOU WANT TO BE A ROCK STAR?
Forgiving a Husband's Betrayal
by Jenny Summers

So here I am. "God, this is beautiful!" I murmured under my breath as I pulled into the driveway of a bed and breakfast nestled between Mount Nittany and Tussey Mountain in central Pennsylvania. This was one of the most breathtaking views of Happy Valley.

Only two days earlier my friend Laura had posed the question, "Jenny, have you had time to make a decision?"

Are your freaking kidding me? I said to myself. "No, Laura. I have three kids and a full-time job. I haven't had time to think. I need to get away." Laura made a phone call, and God graciously provided me with a retreat, a place where I could thoughtfully make a decision and be with him. And I was at the crossroads.

I never pictured myself having to make this kind of decision. I never dreamed that the love of my life would betray me. The past two and a half years had been filled with grief, counseling, lies, giving birth, and then trying to raise three children. I had tried my best to keep my marriage together while crying buckets and buckets of hot tears. I needed time with God because I was about to make the second most important decision of my life.

The most important was the one I had made eight years earlier when I said my vows to Todd on our wedding day. Now I had set out to determine what God wanted me to do about this marriage. I thought I had packed my trusty ol' Bible, but soon realized I hadn't. What was I thinking? I tried to read my "get-your-marriage-back-on-track" books. I couldn't concentrate. So I went for a walk in the neighborhood. The sights were breathtaking. I walked hard and fast. Speaking out loud in this very well-to-do Penn State neighborhood, I said, "God, are you out there? What do you want me to do? My husband has been having an affair for more than two years."

I'm not so sure I've ever heard God before, but I can tell you that I heard my heavenly Father during that walk. The three things I heard were, *I love you. I love Todd. And I hate divorce.* Over and over again these sentences ran through my mind. I couldn't think about anything else.

As the sun set and I breathed in God's goodness, my heart melted. I knew my friends were praying that my heart would soften toward forgiving Todd. I knew there was freedom in forgiveness. For the first time my heart came to the intersection of the choices in front of me. On the left were bright, buzzing, neon signs screaming, "Divorce! Get rid of him! Once a cheater, always a cheater." On the right were the other loud, glaring signs, "Reconcile! Take him back and forgive him!"

Suddenly the way was clear. *If God loves me, he loves Todd, and he hates divorce, what could possibly be against us?* I thought. *How could I, after all these years, give up on my husband?* I prayed for his salvation. I prayed that his heart would soften, and I prayed that his heart would beat only for me.

Was the decision truly this easy? I had seen Todd already making major changes in the way he was living. His heart had changed. He "got it." He was forgiven by Christ, and it oozed from him. He had been sad, angry, and bitter for so long, but he had changed. How could I turn my back on my new man when he wanted me back?

But my heart was full of anger, black as coal with hatred. I hated what he had done to me. I hated the fact I shed tears for him for so long. I hated that he cheated on me while I was carrying our third child. I knew God needed to cleanse me and heal the dark places in my heart. But how?

As it became clear to me what road I needed to take, the burden of having to make decisions about my future became lighter. The road to divorce became more distant. If God hated something, why would I want to do it? How could I ever justify divorcing my husband to my children, especially if God hates it? I had made my choice.

The road to the right looks pretty good, I thought. The road to the left, I knew, would pass desert lands filled with anger, more betrayal, gorges of finan-cial difficulties, brokenness, custody battles, and the possibility of sharing my children with another woman someday. I couldn't bear those thoughts. The road to the right, I knew, had God's bountiful blessings, an intact family, lakes of lessons about forgiveness, mountains to climb to learn how to trust, and plush valleys of rejuvenation and learn-ing about marriage. One road led to despair, the other to life.

During the next few weeks, God used my friend Laura and her husband, Ryan, to show us that it was time to reconcile. It was hard to allow my heart to love again. But it was so good to feel loved by my husband again. His heart beat only for me. I knew Todd wanted to be my husband and the father of our children. When I looked into his eyes, I looked into the eyes of a new man. The day I chose to take the road less traveled, we became cleansed, free, and forgiven.

SO YOU WANT TO BE A ROCK STAR?
Forgiving Your Abuser
by Andrea Hogue

Statistics tell us that one in six American women are victims of sexual assault (see www.rainn.org). It baffles me that such a tragic experience is so common.

When I was in second grade, I was sexually abused by the father of one of my best friends. The abuse happened every time I went to her house to spend the night. Being so young, I did not understand what was happening and was terrified to say anything. Eventually I was able to tell my mom, who was then able to protect me from the abuse. As a single mother she was advised not to take any legal action. He was a prominent man in the community, and Mom was told that her word against his would end up being more damaging to me then just walking away from it. Therefore, in my mind, it became the thing I needed to hide—and hide from—for many years.

I accepted Jesus Christ as my Lord and Savior in my early teens. Through my church experience I was taught about forgiveness—the forgiveness I needed to receive and the forgiveness I needed to dish out to those who had hurt me. Still, I had a relatively immature understanding of forgiveness. I knew I needed to forgive my abuser because Jesus said so. I also heard that if I did not forgive him, I would be allowing my abuser to have control over me, making me bitter and hardened until I let it go. At that point forgiving my abuser had much more to do with me than it had to do with Jesus. Regardless of my motivation, I was trying to walk in forgiveness toward this man.

I married a wonderful, godly man when I was 20. I became the mother of a beautiful baby girl when I was 22. As I moved through life, the wound of abuse would open at different times in different forms. I struggled with feelings of shame, fear, worthlessness, and hopelessness.

Despite all of that I somehow began to believe I had taken care of at least part of my healing. I was really good at ignoring pain and putting on my strong "of-course-I'm-fine-I've-already-dealt-with-this" face. But somewhere inside I think I knew that the only way I would ever find peace was to find a way to forgive my abuser and then trust that my heavenly Father had the power to heal me.

One Sunday my husband and I decided to visit the church I had attended during my teenage years. It was a safe place for me, full of people I loved and who loved me. We dropped off our baby girl in the nursery and then went to enjoy the worship service. As we waited for the service to begin, my abuser entered the room and sat directly in front of us.

You can imagine the fear that overtook me at that point. I nearly vomited from the shock, shame, and disgust I felt. I froze. My husband, Chris, had never seen this man before and had no idea that the individual sitting in front of us was the man whom he felt such rage toward. In my frozen state I mustered up the guts to lean over to Chris and tell him. Chris' body tensed up, and I wanted to hide. The service went on as usual, but my heart and my emotions were not at all "as usual."

The service closed with communion. I went through the motions of getting my bread and juice. Then I was overwhelmed with the thought that I was sharing communion with my abuser. What did that mean? I cannot express how heartsick I felt. I wondered what kind of forgiveness I had for this man and how that affected my belief about Christ's sacrifice. Was I willing to serve a God who would forgive someone like that? The same God who I believed loved me would allow a man as sexually perverse as him to participate in a worship service? In communion? For a split second I wanted to walk away from the cross and say, "No. I would rather serve a God who validates my pain by denying salvation and grace to that sinner." The pride that came from my pain had deceived me. I believed I was more deserving, more worthy to receive the body and blood of Christ than my abuser.

Thankfully the Holy Spirit was also very much

alive in me at that moment. Through the Spirit I realized Christ is the only one truly blameless, yet he suffered a torturous fate to overcome my sin. Both of our sins—mine and my abuser's—hung Jesus on the cross.

If I was going to proceed with taking communion, I had to forgive my abuser and view him as a precious child of God with whom I would one day share eternal life with God. My pride had to die, or the cross of Christ would be meaningless for me.

I took communion that day in a puddle of tears, resting in the strong arms of my husband. It was a perfect picture of all God had already redeemed for me through his grace.

That day I finally understood the greater depth of forgiveness, and through the power of the Holy Spirit, I chose to forgive my abuser. I chose freedom.

"So if the Son sets you free, you will be free indeed." (John 8:36)

TRACK SEVEN: "SUPERSTAR"

TRACK SEVEN: SUPERSTAR

> You may not make the walk of fame
>
> A star may never wear your name
>
> But you will always be
>
> The lead inside His dream
>
> Way before you ever knew
>
> A bigger plan included you
>
> It's not that hard, if you just try
>
> Cause you and I were made to shine

I think I was still running. I was on my way to Africa with a group of other college students for a semester abroad, and I was not going to see my closest friends or family for four months. I started having a minor sense of panic—maybe I hadn't prayed enough. Maybe I was too impulsive. Maybe I can still back out.

My first morning in Africa, I woke up to Dona Alice—I know that's a crazy name, but she was my African mentor and professor—screaming, "There are buffalo! Come see the buffalo!" I woke up facing a wall, not even knowing where I was. Fifty feet away from me herds of elephant and buffalo were feeding. Suddenly it hit me: *Oh my goodness. I'm in Africa. I don't know these people.*

The next four months felt like a deprogramming from American culture. We don't intend it to be this way, but we Americans grow up as captives of our little American "world." The message many of us end up learning is loud and clear: *Our way is the right way. It's the only way.* Being the minority in Africa was a great instructor. The Africans have their own ways of doing things that work for them.

I saw people living in houses with dirt walls and leaves for a ceiling. They woke up with the sun and took care of their families with what little they had. Three-quarters of each day was spent preparing food. Just getting the fire started sometimes took an hour. By the time a meal was cooked and consumed, there maybe was an hour before preparations for the next meal had to begin. But these people seemed so happy, so content. In America we have everything, yet we want more. Soon I realized I was living in the collision of two worlds.

The concept of tribal marriage really threw me. We met with every family group in the village, spending each afternoon with a different family. Each family was polygamous. The family I worked with consisted of one husband, four wives, and 22 kids. I had to know how they functioned like that. They had their own compound. Each wife had her own hut, and the kids she had birthed stayed with her. "Don't you ever get jealous?" I wanted to know. They smiled, shrugged their shoulders, and said, "No, we got over that."

Our host families got a kick out of us. "How come you don't know how to hoe fields? Don't you have a field you hoe at home? Why don't you know how to kill a chicken? Don't you eat chicken?" I found myself completely incapable of explaining grocery stores to these people—the common word pictures I needed simply didn't make sense to them. Try to explain air conditioning or refrigeration to someone who has never used a machine. Yet in my world everything is a machine. I wouldn't have a job without a machine. I don't know that this is the most profound thought I've ever had, but I began to think, *You know, it is only because I was born where I was that I've known the life I've known.* It made me stand more in awe of our God.

I would stand outside in the vast African countryside and stare open-mouthed at the stars. I've never seen so many stars. And I would breathe a prayer: I know and love a God who holds all this in his hand. *How could I ever have been so self-consumed?*

CHOOSE YOUR PLAYLIST: STRENGTH OR POWER?

I wonder if there was ever a time in my life when I was more of a superstar than my four months in Africa. God has given me a lot of really cool opportunities through my music. They say everyone has her 15 minutes of fame. Yes, it's been fun so far to write and record music, to tour, and to sign autographs, but it's so easy to arrive at a place of comfort and say, "Ah, look where my talents and hard work have brought me." Yet if that's an easy place of comfort, then no, thank you. I don't even want to take a nap there.

One of the greatest gifts I received from my time in Africa was the chance to realize how small I truly am. Human beings are pretty insignificant in the long run. We don't choose the century into which we are born, our economic status, our country of origin, whether we are healthy or at risk for a deadly disease. Nearly 210,000 people are born into this world each day. Around 150,000 per day leave. Though we may leave a legacy—a disease healed, an award won, a record set—within one generation our best efforts will most likely be forgotten or bested. I'm not trying to depress anyone. In fact all of these truths ultimately lead to exceedingly good news. Just imagine if these could be newspaper stories:

Man's Decrease Equals God's Increase!

"He must become greater; I must become less. The one who comes from above is above all; the one who is from the earth belongs to the earth, and speaks as one from the earth. The one who comes from heaven is above all."

—JOHN THE BAPTIST (JOHN 3:30-31)

God Made Perfect in Human Weakness!

"But he said to me, 'My grace is sufficient for you, for my power is made perfect in weakness.' Therefore I will boast all the more gladly about my weaknesses, so that Christ's power may rest on me. That is why, for Christ's sake, I delight in weaknesses, in insults, in hardships, in persecutions, in difficulties. For when I am weak, then I am strong."

—THE APOSTLE PAUL (2 CORINTHIANS 12:9-10)

My good friend Janet has stumbled upon this pretty cool concept about the "ins" and the "uns" of being human. Here are the basics: You have an enemy who basically hates your guts. His name is Satan and he loves to poke you—when you're looking, when you're not, when you expect it, when you don't, when you're up, when you're down. He doesn't care. As long as he can draw a little blood here and there, the game stays alive and at least mildly interesting for him. The "ins" and "uns" are one of his favorite playgrounds. They are the perfect setup for the kill. They sound something like this:

You are *in*significant. You are *un*skilled. You are *in*articulate.

You are *un*loved. You are *in*sufficient. You are *un*known.

You are *in*capable. You are *un*done. You are *in*adequate.

Without Christ in our lives, these things are all true. Humans were born from the dust and to the dust we will return. The average man or woman will never achieve fame or infamy. The "ins" and the "uns" leave us feeling as though we have no purpose in life. They are lonely words that foster hopelessness if we listen to them.

But here is the secret to being a superstar. The

moment we own up to the fact that those words could describe us apart from Jesus—I am insufficient to do this on my own. I am unable to finish. I am insecure all the time.—Jesus shows up with this unbelievable sledgehammer of truth and annihilates the enemy. When we are at our most "in" and "un," he is strongest.

Even though our greatest wisdom is foolishness to God, he has decided to endow us with everything that belongs to Jesus. That means we can achieve wisdom that is beyond our experience. At times we may literally radiate the love of Jesus Christ. I once hugged a friend, and she said that as I was praying for her, she had this wonderful feeling that it was not my arms around her, but the actual physical arms of Jesus. We can lead people to God by serving just as well as by preaching. That's what Jesus came to do—to serve. The "ins" and "uns" may be true in the middle of the daily grind, but God relates to us eternally. God is less concerned with our daily failures than with our forever excellence.

He has new names for us to replace the "ins" and the "uns."

You are my child. You are my co-laborer. You are my bride.

You are my friend. You are my ambassador. You are my witness.

You can do all things when I supply you with my strength.

That's why I think Africa allowed me to be a superstar. I was so far out of my comfort zone, so far removed from the ability to claim responsibility for any good I was able to do. I was weak. I was disoriented. And then God showed up. Superstar!

Your song

Get out there and serve somebody today. Forget about all those things you would put on a list called "Things I'm Good At." Instead keep your eyes wide open, looking for somebody who has a need—it won't take very long. Then quietly, humbly, go meet that need. It's even fine if your gift goes unnoticed or is anonymous in nature. Being thanked is far from the goal here.

Earlier we visited the idea that Jesus came not to be served, but to serve (Matthew 20:28). Because we are made in the image of God, we too are created to serve others. In the 1970s Harvard psychologist David McClelland did an experiment that tells us a lot about how we are wired. McClelland showed his test group a film about the selfless giving of Mother Teresa of Calcutta. Some in the test group said they admired Mother Teresa. Others said they had no interest in her or her work. A few did not even know in advance who she was. Yet 100 percent of those who watched the film showed an increase in salivary IgA antibodies, which are produced to strengthen the body's immune system. I see this as evidence that we are created for compassion and care for others. Dr. McClelland himself said, "Dwelling on love seems to strengthen this aspect of immune function" (New York Times, July 22, 1986).

God's desire for our wholeness reaches into every part of our well-being. Part of our choice to follow him and walk like winners is the willingness to lose. Lose your free time; lose your time off; lose your need to be first. Now that's the legacy of a superstar.

SO YOU WANT TO BE A ROCK STAR?

Seventeen Years Old and on My Own
by Nerissa Eimer

"Mommy has cancer." The trembling voice was my father's.

Now I don't know about your experience, but being 12 already wasn't the easiest time of life for me. Throw in a disease, changing schools, and knowing your future is likely to be devastating—it doesn't sound like an easy ride, does it?

As soon as I heard those words come out of my dad's mouth, all I could think was that my mom was going to die, and soon. I didn't even stop to think that she might survive. The only thing my selective hearing took in was *she's dying*. I've always been a negative thinker seeing the half-empty side of life, so when I was faced with a situation that stirred up so much turmoil, as you can probably guess, I didn't feel any hope.

I had already been through a lot in my life. My parents had divorced. I'd moved a few times. As early as I can remember, I had grasped the concept that life isn't fair. But I never thought something as horrible as this would come along to assault my family. I began questioning my faith. *Why should I believe in God if he's going to do this to my family and me? What did we do to deserve this? If I keep believing in him, will he continue to hurt me?* I had so many questions.

I had just left my safe, protected, parochial school and was starting a local public school. Fortunately I became involved with a group called Campus Ministries. I remember telling my youth director what was happening and him telling me not to fear, that God would be with me. Still I was completely distracted as my mom remained sick throughout those middle school and high school years. In so many ways my mom's illness was the perfect opportunity for me to grow closer to God, to learn how to lean on God in the middle of my struggles. But I chose to stay negative, to keep myself preoccupied so I didn't have to think too much about what was really happening.

I did lose my mom at the end of my junior year of high school. And as hard as it was, I was able to cope with the loss because of God. He filled me with strength I didn't have on my own. I don't know how or why, but God's grace stayed with me throughout those six years of Mom's illness. When I look back I can see the ways God protected me, comforted me, and even used my denial to help me deal with everything at my own pace.

Last fall I began college. I am only 17, but I'm pretty independent. I have a job and live in an apartment with a friend. If you've never lived on your own, then this might sound like nothing but fun. And it's true—sort of. Living without parental supervision gives me a lot of freedom. I'm constantly surrounded by pressure from other people my age to go out and party, which entails doing things I don't want to do, things that don't agree with my morals. Although I have the choice to do pretty much anything I want, what I want most is to live by God's will. I have chosen to use this time in my life to become closer to God.

I am embracing God's amazing goodness and might. I never realized just how unfathomable his love, support, and embrace are until now. By choosing not to follow the wrong path as many of my friends have, I have triumphed. On a recent ministry retreat, I came across a verse I think I've known all along: "But whoever listens to me will live in safety and be at ease, without fear of harm" (Proverbs 1:33). I now refer to it constantly and know God has shown it to me it for a reason.

Being on my own and missing my mom, I tend to get lonely. I know my family and friends are here for me, but sometimes it just doesn't make a difference. These are the times when I can't let the Devil drag my spirit down. So I hold on to that verse. By following God, remembering he is with me, and listening to what he says, I am at ease.

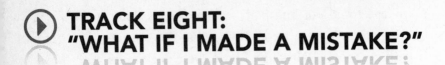

TRACK EIGHT:
"WHAT IF I MADE A MISTAKE?"

> What if I made a mistake?
>
> What if I heard you but
>
> I ignored you?
>
> How many tries will it take?
>
> What if I made a mistake?

I wrote a song while in Africa, a catchy little tune. I was probably still running from a career in music to some degree, but I picked up a guitar to pass the time.

Music still made something inside me light up. I had tried to put it aside in the name of humility for so long that as the longing for music intensified once again in my heart, I didn't know how to respond.

When I came back from Africa, I played that catchy song for my friend Simon. He said, "We're going to record that song." Still, it wasn't until a Saturday morning in April 2005 that I finally came face-to-face with a big choice.

I woke up in my dorm room earlier than expected with a knot in my stomach. I guess you could say my spirit was not at peace. I pulled out my journal because that's what I do when I'm trying to process. And so often that's where God speaks to me. Once again I knew God was asking me to surrender my music, but this was confusing. I had been in a state of surrender for the past two years, doing nothing to pursue fame or glory as a musician. As we talked I began to get a clearer picture of what God required.

This is different. I need you to admit your passion for it. Then I want you to lay it at my feet and remove your hands from it.

The beauty of journaling is the ability to save thoughts and emotions and to reflect on them later, seeing how you've grown and changed. Reading back over that morning entry, I now laugh at my stubborn will fighting to avoid waving the white flag of surrender. Here is what I wrote: "I can't do this by my own strength; I don't even know where to start. If music is something you have in your plan for me, then open the doors, and I will try to be faithful to walk through them as I see them opening." I was still not able to flat out say, "Here, God. Take over."

The date of this epic wrestling match for control over my future was also audition day for the annual Battle of the Bands at my college. The students plan and operate the Agape Music Festival each spring, and three winners from Battle of the Bands get to play on festival stages. I had no intention of auditioning. Those earlier wounds still felt fresh. Could I possibly do this music thing again without losing sight of all I had gained since giving it up?

I planned on treating the day like any other college Saturday. I wandered to the dining hall for breakfast in my usual weekend attire—flannel pants and an old T-shirt. I hadn't showered and probably wouldn't until Monday morning. Midafternoon I made my way over to the band auditions to support a few of my friends. And I discovered that one act had dropped out. I was given the option of filling in, but I had to be ready in five minutes. Once more I stood at a crossroads.

I remembered a promise I'd made to myself—and God—just a few hours earlier: "I will try to be faithful to walk through the doors as I see them opening." This time I knew I wasn't in this for the fame, but because I had a song to sing, an idea to share. I could feel God saying, *Yes. This is what I want for you.*

"Simon?" I found him fiddling with a guitar just off stage. "I was wondering if you could do me a favor."

"I don't think so, Steph. Look. We haven't rehearsed anything; you don't even have a band. Do you have any idea what you're getting into?"

Fortunately I am capable of making a really good pouty face when I need to. I knew it would cause Simon to go against his better judgment. And five minutes later he stood in the shadows of the stage playing a barely rehearsed version of my Africa song. If I had thought about it for any amount of time, logic would have said *No. This is ridiculous. Don't embarrass yourself.*

As crazy as it sounds, I found myself a few weeks later on the main stage in front of the Agape Festival crowd. (Somehow Simon and I had managed to put together some guys for a band and had rehearsed the snot out of our five allotted songs.) I felt as if I was functioning at my best onstage. The world felt like it was spinning right again. We covered an MxPx song, which was a lot of fun for me, and then we played a couple of originals. And offstage, something was developing that changed my world from that moment on.

As I was playing my short set, a tour bus was pulling up in the receiving area behind the stage. Several musicians hopped off the bus and headed backstage to see who was performing. After my final song I exited the stage, flying from the adrenaline rush. The first person to introduce himself was a guy named Todd, TobyMac's bass player. I think our initial exchange may have fit the Cartoon Network quite well.

Todd was as cool as could be. "Hey. We really liked your sound. You have any demos we could buy? I'd like Toby to hear your stuff."

I, on the other hand, was a blithering idiot. "Do you think I could meet him?" There was no thank you—no realization that a door into the music world was cracking open before me. This was just something I could cross off my 100-things-to-do-before-you-die list: Meet TobyMac. I had no other expectations. The guys bought several demos and told me they would see me around. In three seconds flat I was on the phone—there were a lot of people who would never believe this story.

Hyper-excitement aside, I had only one more hour before I would have to leave my make-believe rock star world and rejoin the ranks of the Agape volunteers in our matching T-shirts. I thought I would hit the hospitality tent for a quick bite, see if any bands were hanging out in there, and then get back to work. It was a little crowded. There was a guy in a pink shirt. I heard him excuse himself, step right in front of me, and say, "Excuse me, Stephanie. I'm Toby."

My first thought was that somebody was playing a joke on me. Then I realized it really was Toby. I gasped and immediately became exceedingly animated. "You are Toby! Oh, I'm a huge fan." I was pumping his hand up and down—it looked like an oil rig on steroids.

Toby kind of took me under his wing throughout the day. I did my festival chores, but he was around. I shared a little about going to Africa. I was honest with him—this was very new for me. It was my first performance in almost two years. But God had reconfirmed in my life that this was what he wanted me to be doing. The bus was rolling out at 11 that night when Toby called to me a final time. "Let's stay in touch. Hey, my advice to you is this: Don't be in a hurry to find a record deal. You're really young. Don't take the first deal offered to you." And they were gone.

Here's some irony. The first deal I was offered was a development deal from TobyMac and Gotee records. I will not be dishonest. My reaction to the offer was nothing short of a good old-fashioned freakout. After my friends peeled me from the ceiling, I remembered what Toby had said. "You're really young. Don't take the first deal offered to you."

What in the world, Toby? Which "you" do I listen to?

It was hard, but ultimately the whole situation made me pay attention to what the Holy Spirit was saying to me in my gut. I took Toby's advice. It made more sense to say, "Hey, can you guys wait until I close out this season of my life? Let me wrap up school; then I'll be all yours."

I convinced myself for about an evening that I had made the right decision, but I couldn't arrive at peace about it. I wanted the peace. I would pay for peace! *Come on, God. Would it hurt to give me a little peace?* But it just didn't come.

My decision to finish school dramatically slowed my reentry into the music scene. It wasn't like my career picked up right where I had left it the day I held off on Toby's initial offer. There was a point where I was pretty low. I can't tell you how many times I thought, I made a mistake, didn't I?

Even after I finished school and signed a record deal, it took a long time to get the career wheels turning. There has been a truckload of character-building involved—I worked hard for a year, figuring out insurance, learning to pay rent, splitting time between the studio and Starbucks, and figuring out how to be far more patient than I knew how to be. But mostly I have been learning not to judge the restless soul. Man, sometimes when I read the stories of Israel—how they constantly doubted God and questioned God's decisions—I think, After all that Israel had seen, how could they forget? How could they lose sight? Let me tell you, we are people who need constant confirmation.

CHOOSE YOUR PLAYLIST:
BEST DEAL OR FIRST DEAL?

What if I made a mistake? How many times have you said those words? Better yet, how many times have you said those words today? Why is it that in the middle of receiving exactly what we thought we wanted from God, we panic? The manna is falling from heaven like a blizzard of blessing, and we're watching in disdain, wishing we could go back to our stale bread.

The Israelites had been imprisoned in Egypt for 400 years. During that time they built entire cities for pharaohs under the cruel threat of the whip. But throughout the enslavement of Israel, God continued to make his blessings evident—even to the Egyptians. So the Egyptians increased their cruelty. Pharaoh demanded that Hebrew baby boys be put to death. When Hebrew and Egyptian midwives alike refused this task, Pharaoh gave all of Egypt the command to put to death any Hebrew baby boy they saw. Pharaoh's goal was to keep Israel enslaved. He figured if he got rid of the boys, there would eventually be fewer men to attempt a revolt.

You know how that part of the story ends. God sent plague upon plague to Egypt, and Pharaoh finally released the Israelites. And off they went on their own incredible journey.

God's grace to the people was abundant. Water flowed from rocks. Bread fell from the sky. And as quickly as God had parted a mighty sea to allow Israel to cross on dry ground, they forgot how bad it had been to be mercilessly enslaved by a people who wanted to see them destroyed. "At least we had food in Egypt!" they cried. "Remember the fish we used to eat? Remember the leeks, onions, cucumbers, melons? Mmm, and the garlic?"

Yet God kept providing. Manna surrounded them every morning, and God instructed the people to gather only what they needed for each day. But of course the people didn't believe there would be more manna in the morning, so they hoarded what they had. This irked God. The next morning, instead of having a little secret stash of manna, the people had maggots and a rotten smell to deal with. That's right, the manna rotted. If they had listened, if they had trusted, if they had remembered God's goodness, they would have had everything they needed—and then some. (You can read the whole story in Exodus 16).

Do you remember the classic commercial for Tootsie Pops where the wise old owl poses the question, "How many licks does it take to get to the center of a Tootsie Pop?" We never find out—everyone who tries to count, including the wise owl, is overcome by their zeal for the Tootsie Roll at the center of the pop, and they bite into it. How long did it take Israel to forget God's provision? Less than a chapter.

As the people arrived at the Promised Land—the place God told them to go—their own spies reported that it was a no-go. "There are already people there, and they're too big to fight," they said. "They're giants. There's no way we can possess this land." And at once the people wailed a familiar lament: "We never should have left Egypt."

Do you have the patience to be out there in the desert? Do you have the faith to believe that when God makes a promise, he can and will follow through? I think Satan can actually weasel his way into the picture through one of two routes here. He can tell us it's too hard to follow God, that there's no way we could ever have what God has promised. That's the one that snagged Israel. Or he can suggest it will be easy. It's kind of the reverse psychology principle. If we begin believing that we have it made, we don't prepare. We let our guard down, and suddenly, we are easy targets for pride, greed, and laziness. Promises of ease are neither true nor godly.

Listen, rather, to these promises from the Bible:

"But seek first his kingdom and his

righteousness,

and all these things will be given to you as well.

Therefore do not worry about tomorrow, for

tomorrow will worry about itself. Each day has

enough trouble of its own."

(Matthew 6:33-34)

"In this world you will have trouble. But take

heart! I have overcome the world."

(John 16:33)

"But he said to me, 'My grace is sufficient for you, for my power is made perfect in weakness.' Therefore I will boast all the more gladly about my weaknesses, so that Christ's power may rest on me. That is why, for Christ's sake, I delight in weaknesses, in insults, in hardships, in persecutions, in difficulties. For when I am weak, then I am strong." (2 Corinthians 12:9-10)

Difficulty is not necessarily a sign you've made a mistake. Difficulty is a sign you are still alive and sucking in air. But God uses the difficult, slow, and frustrating times in our lives to build character and prepare us for the promises that lie ahead.

If we wait patiently on the Lord, he uses those times of difficulty to peel back all of the layers of scales, dirt, and disuse that have accumulated on our eyes. For years I bore a wound from the first words my father had spoken to me. As I took the long, slow walk toward where God was leading me, God revealed to me how he long had been preparing me for this new part of my life:

He had been teaching me to speak blessings, not curses.

He had been teaching me to praise him through my desert times.

He had been teaching me to talk when I felt like shutting down.

He had been teaching me about beauty and his intentional design.

He had been teaching me to settle the issue of fame—God gets the glory.

He had been teaching me about loving without conditions.

He had been teaching me about serving like a superstar.

Now, at last, there were some new first words that had come my way, words that launched me into the life God had been preparing me for. "Excuse me, Stephanie?" he said. I didn't realize the importance of Toby's first words until I began putting my entire story together. He said my name.

Born Stephanie, I once lost my name. And maybe you, too, have lost yourself somewhere in this big world. But God knows you by name, and he longs to restore you. You'll see.

 ## Your song

Put some worship music on your MP3 player and find a nice hiking trail somewhere. Hike deep into the woods and find a spot to rest—a place that you find beautiful and inspiring. Then simply ask God to talk to you. Be sure when you return home that you journal his first words to you.

SO YOU WANT TO BE A ROCK STAR?

What If God Asks Me to Move?
by Rachael Poss

A typical weekend for my best friend and me was going to a movie, probably with boys, then hanging out downtown until late, sleeping at her house, and then going out all day Saturday. We often ended up watching music videos and dancing around. We had so much fun together in California. Her home was like my second home. Our friendship was one of the things I hung onto during some of the hardest times in my life. And now I would have to say good-bye. I found out I soon would move to Pennsylvania. California and Pennsylvania are like completely different worlds. And really, it wouldn't have mattered if I were moving across the state or across the country. I was going to leave my home, my friends, and everything I knew.

My sister and I had been living with a foster family, and after much thought and prayer, they decided we weren't the right fit for their family. They just couldn't handle two more daughters. So when I learned my sister and I were moving, I sat in the bathroom crying—longing for a family and fearing that I would never have one.

My friends were the closest thing I had to family. Leaving them was hard for me, but the fact that I was going to have to start over at a new school and meet a new set of strict parents just made it worse. It's not like I was a bad kid. I just didn't like the idea of having people tell me how late I could stay up or checking to make sure I had spent the night at the house where I said I was.

The big day arrived—my last day at Santa Barbara High School. Of course my best friend and I cried. Well, I guess we didn't only cry; we bawled. I remember her saying, "Don't worry, Rachael; you will make friends. You're you. Everyone loves you." To a certain degree I believed her. *She's right,* I thought. I *am going to go to this new high school, make friends, and everything will be okay*

Well it was a nice thought. I'm fairly outgoing. I love people. I love talking to people. But my first week at Penns Valley High School was probably one of the worst weeks of my life. No one talked to me. No one even wanted to know my name or why I was there. The girls thought I wanted to steal their boyfriends, and the boys were just...weird. I spent almost every lunch period in the bathroom crying. I couldn't handle the stress of no one liking me.

I was so mad at God. Why did I have to be here? Why didn't I have any friends? What did I do to cause this?

When my sophomore year started, I left the public school and went to a Christian high school.

It was a totally different environment. People accepted me. They were kind and loving. I finally felt close to God again.

As I look back I can see what God was doing. My best friend in California was an amazing friend, but we made some bad decisions together. If I'd have stayed in California, who knows what would have happened to me. I believe God saved me from a messed-up future. God also gave me friends who loved me and helped me to grow in my relationship with him.

Moving wasn't easy by any means. So many times I wanted to jump on a plane back to California and leave this place that, at the time, felt like the equivalent of sticking toothpicks underneath my toenails and then kicking a soccer ball. But I know God put me here for a reason. He wanted me to run to him. He wanted me to say *Abba, Daddy, please help me*. It took some time, but I finally cried out to God—and my life began to change.

Moving was one of the most difficult things I ever had to do. In my heart I hoped God would be with me in my new home. I hoped God would bless me. And he did. He always does.

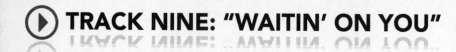
> Another day, another story
>
> A little different this time
>
> It could've ended up the same way
>
> But I learned to give it up instead
>
> It's amazing how it happens
>
> When I just let you take control
>
> I don't need saving from myself

Communication with my dad—the first since I was 19—started again right after Father's Day the year I turned 22. I think I was responding to all those Father's Day ads I saw on television. Suddenly I felt sensitive to "father things" again. *Hmm, I thought I had taken care of this,* I mused. *I guess I'll just pray for my dad.*

And then God gave me a word for my dad: Purpose. I had no idea what that meant. I hadn't talked to my dad in three years. All I had was an old e-mail address, and I had no idea if it would work any longer. But I thought I'd give it a shot. I jotted him a quick note.

"Hey, I've been praying for you; you've been on my heart lately. I think God wants you to hear this word, too: Purpose. Does that mean anything to you?"

The next day I had an e-mail back from him.

"How did you know to tell me? How did you know to write?"

After 17 years of driving trucks, my dad had gone back to school and finished his degree in architecture. My daddy is a smart man. Yet two days before I had written to him, he had gone into work—at a very good job—and packed up his desk. He quit. Just like that. He was mortified at what he had done.

He said he would be passing through Nashville, my new home, soon, and he'd love to stop by and see me. The night before we were to meet for the third time in 22 years, I broke down. I was hurting. God has done a lot in my heart, but I still crave a daddy sometimes. But my dad didn't know me. He didn't know he should be proud of me—of my heart, my character. He didn't know what I was passionate about.

It was a deep ache. But you know what? That was okay. God has taught me that it's okay to long for that; when my earthly father can't give me what

I need, my heavenly Father can. I gave myself a little pep talk. *I'm going to see him tomorrow. If we didn't have an arranged spot and time to meet, he'd probably walk right past me and not know who I was. That's my father.*

The next day began with an amazing challenge from God. As I drove to meet my dad, I could feel God's presence, and I knew that no matter what holes my dad might leave in my heart this time, God would fill them up. But that wasn't the challenge. The real test was whether I would let God be, well, God. It was as if God were whispering in my ear: *I am enough. Do you believe that? Are you going to allow me to be enough for you?*

I believe God is tenderhearted and has compassion on me, but I also believe there comes a point where God says, *Okay, this is becoming a pity party. Get out there. You know what to do.*

I pulled up to the Best Western parking lot in my green 1993 Honda Accord. My dad was pacing the parking lot. That was totally him—full of nervous energy. I parked and took a deep breath. Then I exploded from the car and threw my arms around him.

"It's great to see you!" I still didn't quite know what to call him.

"I can't believe you're still driving this car! I'm

going to try to buy you a new car."

The next morning we had breakfast at Shoney's, and he asked me to put together a list of my top five cars. In my mind I was trying to write it all off as empty promises. My heart, however, would not let it go. It was the first time I ever looked him in the eye and truly wanted to tell him I loved him and forgave him. I looked right at him as I spoke.

"I can't really explain it, but I love you. I really do. I know there's a lot unspoken over the last couple of years. I'm just excited that you're sitting in front of me here today." It felt so good to say it.

His face got red, and he swallowed hard. He didn't know how to digest that or respond. He just kind of nodded.

We talked on and off over the next couple of weeks. He called and said he was doing research on cars. Every once in a while I'd call him. Then he figured out how to text. He wrote sweet notes: "God has blessed you with beauty. Okay, there's a double portion here, but who's complaining!" It had never been clearer to me that God had used my relationship with my dad for good. Dad even followed through on his promise of a car—I still drive the one my dad found for me.

Our communication lasted for almost a year this time. As of now, he has backed out again. It's been almost six months since I've heard from him. This time around I have to admit it hurts a little more. Before, he didn't know me. I could always use that as the reason he backed away. But this time we had "invested." He told me more about himself than I'd ever known. He had started to get to know my heart. He did know me.

Once again I'm in some uncharted waters. And once again I have to choose whether or not to forgive my dad. I will have to choose every day for the rest of my life. I do expect him to resurface. But in the meantime I'm loving him from a distance, and he's still blessing me through this car that I couldn't survive without. Right now, that's the love he's able to give me.

No matter what happens, I understand forgiveness. It's unconditional. It's not based on circumstance or emotion. It's something that gets planted by God in good soil. After he waters and tends it, it grows and produces a crop of healing that is 30, 60, 100 times what is sown. When it comes down to it, forgiveness is a story of the soil. Some of us, for some reason, can forgive. Some of us lose that fight.

CHOOSE YOUR PLAYLIST: HEALING OR HURTING?

A horrible thing happened in 2006 in a small Pennsylvania community a couple of hours away from where I grew up. A one-room Amish schoolhouse became the scene of one of the most deadly school shootings in American history. Five little Amish girls were killed execution-style by a horribly confused gunman who killed himself as well. And the whole community, including the families of these precious children, did something astonishing. They forgave the man who murdered their daughters.

The families, who decline to be named in interviews, insist it is community that has permitted them to heal and to forgive.

"I don't know how I would feel if we had been the only ones," said the mother of one of the victims. Shortly after the shootings a number of English families (that is what the Amish call non-Amish neighbors) showed up on the families' doorsteps. These people had also lost children in tragic circumstances. They cried with the Amish community and shared their own stories.

"That was counseling at its best," one Amish father said. "They shared with us how they felt. We saw that's exactly how we feel, and that made us feel a little better." (www.ap.lancasteronline.com).

The Amish families have had a chance to pass along that compassion as well. After the April 16, 2007, shootings at Virginia Tech University, several family members of the slain Amish girls traveled to the VT campus to present what they called a "comfort quilt" to the mourning families there.

And, in perhaps the most stunning display of forgiveness, the New Hope Amish community, which received more than $4 million in gifts to help with medical bills and other needs, set aside a portion of that gift to set up a trust fund for the widow and children of the man who shot the girls at the Amish school. Half of the mourners at the man's small, private funeral were Amish, including the families of the girls whose lives this man had taken.

The group offered an explanation for their display of forgiveness, "You have to have a will to forgive. You have to want to forgive, and that's the first step." (www.ap.lancasteronline.com)

Can everyone forgive? The truly operative word in that question is not the word *forgive*. Rather, it is the word *can*. Is everyone, at some level, *able* to forgive? I have to believe from example and from history that the answer is yes. We are all given the tools necessary to forgive. All we need is the faith to use them.

Jesus said, "If you forgive others when they sin

against you, your heavenly Father will also forgive you. But if you do not forgive others their sins, your Father will not forgive your sins" (Matthew 6:14-15). Logic, of course, leads us to the next question: Would Jesus have said this if it were impossible to forgive?

Jesus sets the standard in everything for you and me. There have been times when my human authority figures have set the bar too high for me. Teachers gave me too much homework to complete. Employers have asked me to work beyond what is physically bearable. Maybe now and then my mom has expected me to react with more maturity than I could muster.

But while Jesus set the bar even higher, he assures us that when he asks us to do something—anything—the tools necessary to do that thing are already within us. The Bible says, "Bear with each other and forgive one another if any of you has a grievance against someone. Forgive as the Lord forgave you." (Colossians 3:13) We are expected to forgive—it's not an option. And it's not too much for us to bear. It might be hard. It might take years. But with God's help it's possible.

One of the Greek words for forgiveness is *chari-zomai*. Though we translate it as forgiveness, it also means to do something pleasant or agreeable for someone; to do a favor. That word tells us that our behavior needs to be gracious and kind. When you look at it that way, it begs the question once again. *Can* everyone be gracious and kind? *Can* everyone be pleasant and agreeable? Now it sounds much more like an actual choice, doesn't it? *Can* and *will* are at times such completely different words. Yes, everyone can do these things.

Forgiveness is a choice. It is rarely easy, but the right choices rarely are—even fewer are easy to carry out. Part of living like an adult is realizing that the prize doesn't always show up during the journey. Look at life like a race—after all, that's the picture Scripture paints for us (take a look at 1 Corinthians 9:24 and Hebrews 12:1). While the race is being run, there are no ribbons, trophies, or medals being distributed to the runners. The winners have yet to be determined. During the race there is hardship. Bodies strain and ache. Muscles pull, and dehydration threatens to destroy the athlete's system. Every athlete knows there is pain in the course of the race. Sometimes the only physical response the winners can muster is to weep. This is why even the spectators feel a rush of adrenaline watching athletes compete.

The victor is not the one who feels no pain. The winner is not the one who has avoided every obstacle. The trophy does not often end up in the hands of a rookie. Experience trumps youth almost every time. Life can be such an uphill battle. What was it that Bible commentator Matthew Henry said once again? "To expect unchanging happiness in a changing world, must end in disappointment."

In many ways our emotional wholeness also comes down to a choice. The Word of God unflinchingly relates forgiveness to healing. James 5 speaks to the emotions. It says that when we are troubled, we should pray. When we are happy, we should sing praise songs. And when we are sick, we should call our elders to pray over us. "And the prayer offered in faith will make them well; the Lord will raise them up. If they have sinned, they will be forgiven. Therefore confess your sins to each other and pray for each other so that you may be healed. The prayer of a righteous person is powerful and effective" (James 5:15-16).

C.S. Lewis wrote, "God, who foresaw your tribulation, has specially armed you to go through it, not without pain but without stain" (W.H. Lewis, 219). You and I are armed. We have all the tools we need to make a choice, to run a good race, and to come through victorious in the end. But it is a choice.

In some ways this book has been the story of a dad and his girl. It is the tale of an unresolved relationship wrought with pain, false starts, and uncertainty, but seasoned with love, longing, and promise. There is no telling what the end of this story will be for my dad and me. But I know it will work together for good as long as I stay attached to Jesus. That's all I know.

If you draw breath and are in relationship with even one other human being, then this book has been your story every bit as much as it has been mine. You have choices to make every day. At times you may become confused in defining those choices. You might think those choices are the obvious ones sitting in front of you:

Do I choose to live with Mom or Dad now?

Should I even try to develop a new reputation after all the lousy things I have done?

Am I going to put my heart out there to get broken again?

But the real choices are the bigger, deeper, longer lasting ones: the choices about who you will trust to guide your life, about what you will believe with regard to forgiveness, about who gets the privilege of receiving your greatest devotion. Those are the choices that will make you who you are and who you want to be.

Your song

I want to suggest a simple concept to you. All choices come down to one thing. Do I trust that God is who he says he is and that I am who he says

I am? All other questions take our eyes off the real story. The author of Hebrews talked about running a race. (Paul also did this at least four times in his letters—maybe these guys were marathon runners.) Hebrews 12:1-2 says, "And let us run with perseverance the race marked out for us, fixing our eyes on Jesus, the pioneer and perfecter of faith."

What would happen if we fixed our eyes on Jesus rather than our circumstances? What if at each crossroads, rather than asking, "What am I going to do about *this*?" we asked, "Well, God, what are you going to do with this one? Who are *you* again, God? I really need to remember."

He is your friend.

He is your Daddy.

He is your strong tower and your refuge.

He is all-powerful, all-knowing, and present everywhere.

He loves you.

He has made a way for you—Jesus.

He is enough.

His mercies are new every morning.

He gives, and he takes away.

He commands the winds and the waves.

He has gone to prepare a place for you.

He is coming back.

"And who am I? Tell me again..."

You are more than a conqueror.

You are fearfully and wonderfully made.

You are created in the image of the living God.

You are his ambassador.

You are his beloved.

You are the sheep of his pasture.

You are his bride.

You once were lost, but now you are found.

You are a captive who has been set free.

You are no longer ruled by sin and death.

You are a new creation.

Our lives will continue to bring us to crossroads. For everything there is a season and a time for every purpose under heaven. What will you do the next time you stand at a crossroads? My prayer is that you will choose to trust in the God who loves you, who will never leave you, who will fill up all the empty places inside you. I'm pulling for you—I need you pulling for me as well.

"This day I call heavens and earth as witnesses against you that I have set before you life and death, blessings and curses. Now choose life, so that you and your children may live." (Deuteronomy 30:19)

TRACK ONE: "LOVE OUT LOUD"

 Works Cited

Advocates for Youth, "Child Sexual Abuse 1: An Overview," 1995, www.advocatesforyou.org/PUBLICATIONS/factsheet/fsabuse1.htm

Americans for Divorce Reform, "Divorce Statistics Collection," www.divorcereform.org/rates.html

ANRED: Anorexia Nervosa and Related Eating Disorders, Inc., "Statistics: How Many People Have Eating Disorders?" 2005, www.anred.com/stats.html

Darwin, CR. *The Origin of Species By Means of Natural Selection.* 6th ed. London: Senate, 1994.

Fathers for Life, www.fathersforlife.org/divorce/chldrndiv.htm

Hammond, Frank D. *The Father's Blessing.* Plainview, Texas: The Children's Bread Ministry, 2001.

The HTML Bible, "Matthew Henry's Commentary: Ecclesiastes 3," www.htmlbible.com/kjv30/henry/H21C003.htm

Lewis, C.S., *The Problem of Pain,* New York: Macmillan, 1960.

Lewis, W.H., ed. *Letters of C.S. Lewis.* New York: Harcourt Brace Jovanovich, 1966.

Stauffer, Cindy, and Ad Crable, "Amish Girls' Parents Talk of Loss, Faith, Survival." *Lancaster Online,* September 27, 2007, www.ap.lancasteronline.com /4/pa_exchange_amish_shooting